D1426918

Studies in Semiotics

Sign and Subject
Semiotic and Psychoanalytic Investigations Into Poetry
Daniel Laferrière

The Peter de Ridder Press

STUDIES IN SEMIOTICS

edited by Thomas A. Sebeok

Research Center for Language and Semiotic Studies
Indiana University

Volume 14

DANIEL LAFERRIÈRE

SIGN AND SUBJECT

Semiotic and Psychoanalytic Investigations Into Poetry

LISSE

THE PETER DE RIDDER PRESS

1978

ISBN 90 316 0138 1

Printed in Great Britain by H Charlesworth & Co Ltd

Preface

The aim of this book is to apply insights from semiotics and psychoanalysis to poetry. In so doing I hope not only to contribute to the science of poetics, but also to shed some light on how semiotics and psychoanalytic theory can themselves be related to one another. If I were to state my aim in terms of the two most important influences upon my research, I would say that this book reaches toward a synthesis of the linguistic semiotics initiated by Roman Jakobson with the psychoanalytic psychology invented by Sigmund Freud. Elsewhere (Laferrière 1977B) I have used the epithet 'psycholinguistic' in an attempt to describe the combination of linguistic and psychoanalytic approaches to poetry.

Some of the chapters of this book have appeared in earlier versions: II (Laferrière 1974), IV (1978b), V (1977a), VI (1976b). I wish to thank the editors of *Semiotica* and *Versus* for their kind permission to print revisions of earlier articles. Chapters I, III, and most of IV appear here for the first time.

I also wish to thank various colleagues, teachers, and friends who have at one point or another provided me with helpful comments: Richard Beck, Sheila Blumstein, Wayles Browne, Michael Bourke, John Casey, Catherine Chvany, Robert Crosman, Armen Dedekian, Sam Driver, Claud DuVerlie, Irene Fairley, Charles Isenberg, Roman Jakobson, Martha Laferrière, Richard Oehrle, Michel Pierssens, Tatiana Roman, John Robert Ross, Barbara Shapiro, Nomi Tamir, Victor Terras, Jean-Jacques Thomas, and Thomas Winner.

Contents

Juggling Poetics, Semiotics, and Psychoanalysis

> ...à coté de la conscience immédiate
> de l'identité entre le signe et l'objet (A
> est A), la conscience immédiate de l'ab-
> sence de cette identité (A n'est pas A)
> est nécessaire. . . .
>
> Roman Jakobson

A *poem* is a peculiar complex of *signs* uttered by a special kind of *subject*. Such a definition is sufficiently broad to apply at least three distinct and relatively advanced bodies of knowledge to the study of poetry: poetics, which has a rich and illustrious history from Aristotle to Jakobson; general semiotics, which achieved its most explosive advance in the writings of Charles Sanders Peirce; and psychology, which deals with the signifying subject in approaches as various as behaviorism, psychoanalysis, gestalt psychology, etc.

The problem with broad definitions, however, is that they are in danger of floundering on details. Precisely how does one relate poetics, semiotics, and psychology? And what schools in these fields does one choose to relate? For example, is it preferable to interpret the linguistic structures in a poem from the viewpoint of Skinner's theory of verbal behavior, or is it better to understand them in the light of Lacan's neo-psychoanalytic notion of "discours de l'Autre?" What does the poetic entropy of information theory have to do with the positive reinforcers of behaviorist theory? How is the psycho-analytic notion of repression related to poetic information? How does the poet manage to signify repressed wishes, and what are the psychological conditions promoting the peculiar kind of semiosis the poet engages in?

There are clearly too many of these difficult interdisciplinary questions to answer in a single book. One cannot hope for, indeed perhaps one should not even desire a monolithic synthesis of poetics, semiotics, and psychology. At this early point it is sufficient merely to puncture the boundaries between the disciplines and hope that scholars in the individual disciplines will not react with territorial defensiveness.

The boundary between semiotics and psychoanalysis offers a particularly interesting area of inquiry. What is the relationship of the sign (as studied by semiotics) and the subject (as studied by psychoanalysis)? An extremely cautious answer to this question has already been provided by Eco:

Insofar as the subject, along with some of its properties and attitudes, is presupposed by the statements, then it has to be 'read' as an element of the conveyed content. Any other attempt to introduce a consideration of the subject into the semiotic discourse would make semiotics trespass one of its 'natural' boundaries. (1976:315)

What is behind, before or after, outside or *too much* inside the methodological "subject" outlined by this book might be tremendously important. Unfortunately it seems to me — at this stage — beyond the semiotic threshold. (1976:317)

But there is a curious contradiction in Eco's solution: if the (desiring, fearing, needing) subject is outside the range of semiotics, why does Eco go to the trouble of defining the subject in specifically semiotic terms? For example:

. . . the most reliable grasp that semiotics can have on . . . subjective activity is the one provided by a theory of codes: *the subject of any semiotic enquiry being no more than the semiotic subject of semiosis, that is, the historical and social result of the segmentation of the world that a survey on Semantic Space makes available.* This subject is a way of looking at the world and can only be known as a way of segmenting the universe and of coupling semantic units with expression-units: by this labor it becomes entitled to continuously destroy and restructure its social and historical systematic concretions. (1976:315)

Apparently, there is some hope after all of dealing with the subject, but only if the subject is semioticized, is himself made into a sign. A sign in fact is just what Peirce thought the subject (the 'interpreter') to be:

It is that the word or sign that man uses IS the man itself ["le style c'est l'homme même" — Buffon]. For, as the fact that every thought is a sign, taken in conjunction that life is a train of thought, proves that man is a sign; so that every thought is an *external* sign, proves that man is an external sign. That is to say, the man and the external signs are identical, in the same sense in which the words *homo* and *man* are identical. Thus my language is the sum total of myself: for the man is the thought. (Peirce, *Collected Papers*, V, 314, as quoted by Eco. 1976:316)

On the one hand Eco is arguing that semiotics is not yet capable of dealing with the signifying subject, while on the other hand he urges that, if semiotics *must* deal with the subject, it must do so semiotically. Perhaps it is best to simply ignore the first part of Eco's argument and concentrate on the benefits of treating the subject from a semiotic perspective. Semiotics, after all, has developed some sophisticated tools (especially the tools of linguistics) for dealing with the subject's signifying practices, and there is no reason why psychology should disregard these tools. Conversely, the field of psychology has a long history of dealing with the subject, and there is no reason why semiotics should not reap the benefits of psychological research. The adjacent disciplines of semiotics and psychology have each advanced too far to permit any more territorial behavior.

We should not, however, pretend that there are *no* distinctions between disciplines. The ability to 'free associate' across· various fields of knowledge, to roam at random, for example, from quasi-grammatological principles to the structure of the unconscious can certainly be stimulating. In the worst cases, however, it can also produce the impression of private babbling on the analyst's couch. There is, no· doubt, a considerable "furieux d'intelligence" in the writers to whom I am referring — e.g., Kristeva, Derrida, Lacan, and others — but, at moments when one has read and reread a particularly difficult passage five or ten times, there is a strong temptation to dismiss the passage as just so much mumbo-jumbo and assorted jargon mongering (cf. Andreski 1972:71-72). Let me emphasize that it is infinitely more interesting to read such explorations than to read, say, a dissertation written in Standard American English Department Style. Kristeva's *La révolution du langage poétique*, for example, is one of the most interesting collections of interdisciplinary ruminations ever written, and it is particularly admirable in its attempt to integrate the subject into the semiotic enterprise (see also Kristeva 1972). But the book cannot in any clear sense be refuted. And it cannot be refuted not because it is 'correct', but because it does not make clear, unambiguous, testable claims. It is simply too rich, semantically — so rich and so suggestive as to be more a literary work of art than a work of analysis (compare Jakobson, whose claims are usually unambiguous and intended to be taken literally). Perhaps what we are witnessing in the work of many of the current French inquirers is a localized literary movement or genre which literary historians of the future will scrutinize with great interest. In the meantime we, mere contemporaries, will have to catch as catch can. That is, we can criticize the 'Parisian School' for its analytic shortcomings, but there is no reason why we should not profit from its suggestiveness. Or, to mix Reikian and Lacanian metaphors, we should learn to listen with our third ear to the discourse of the gaulic Other.

I suggested above that psychology has much to teach the semiotician about the subject. Psychoanalysis in particular has a wealth of insights because many of the signs that semioticians deal with are unconscious. Psychoanalysis is, after all, the science of the unconscious, and its techniques for dealing with unconscious processes ought to be useful in dealing with certain unconscious signifying processes. Of course not all unconscious or unintentional signs have been dealt with by psychoanalysis — e.g., the speaker's proxemic behavior or speech 'accent' which may unconsciously signify his national origin to the listener. But many kinds of unconscious signs have always been of direct interest to psychoanalysis, as for example the unintentional iconic signs that psychoanalysts call "symbols" (Jakobson 1970b:10).

A more important reason for bringing semiotics and psychoanalysis together is a remarkable parallel between the function of the sign and the function of the signifying subject. Consider the very definition of a sign: a sign is something which stands for something else — *aliquid stat pro aliquo*, as the Medieval schoolmen asserted and as later semioticians such as Peirce, Morris, Jakobson, Sebeok, and Eco continued to assert. Implicit in this formulation of the sign is the notion that what the sign stands for is *absent* from the sign. The sign stands for something that is not itself, that is missing. A chair is not present, for example, in the word *chair*. Rather, the word *chair* is by definition not the chair. The verbal sign is in some sense a substitution for the thing signified and can never *be* the thing signified. *Every sign not only stands for what it stands for, but also stands for the absence of what it stands for*. No matter how physically 'real' or 'present' the chair may seem to the speaker at the moment he utters the sign *chair*, the actual chair will still always be absent from that sign. This notion of the sign as an absence ("le signe-absence") has already been recognized as an important aspect of signifying behavior (e.g., Meschonnic 1975:20ff.). The sign-absence has also been related to Freud's well known analysis of the *fort-da* episode in child development, i.e., the stage where the child learns to reconcile itself with the *absence* of the mother (Freud, *Standard Edition of the Complete Psychological Works* [hereafter SE], XVIII, 14ff.; Lacan 1966:276; Meschonnic 1975:316-317). In certain kinds of schizophrenia there is an attempt to escape from the sign-as-absence, i.e., the patient reifies verbal signs to the extent that they no longer denote the *absence* of things signified, but the *presence* of themselves. They become 'things' to be focused upon and played with in such schizophrenic activities as verbigeration and production of "word salad" (Freud captures this pathological reification of verbal signs by saying that the patient hypercathects the *Wortvorstellung* at the expense of the *Dingvorstellung* – SE, XIV, 200-204).

A more moderate and controlled hypercathexis of the *Wortvorstellungen* (read: signifiers) is to be found in the creation and reception of poetry. Such slogans as the Romantic "l'art pour l'art" and the Russian Futurist "slovo kak takovoe" especially reveal an attempt to escape from the sign as an absence and to embrace the sign as an intensified presence of nothing but itself. Such devices as the automorphic structures (below, Ch. II) attract considerable attention toward themselves and away from external reality. The mirror symmetries in particular (e.g., epanalepsis) represent an attempt to isolate the poem from the reality surrounding it, to envelop the poem in a complex of reflexive structures which promote an illusion that the poem refers to nothing but itself.

But to return to our comparison of the sign and the subject: in the same way that the sign is an absence, the subject of any signifying behavior is also an absence. The subject is, after all, as absent from the things (referents) he signifies as are the signs he uses. Like the sign, the subject cannot be what is signified, the subject cannot *be* the object. Both the subject and the sign are in what the linguist would call a privative opposition to the thing signified: [− presence of referent] vs. [+ presence of referent]. Both sign and subject are *negative* elements from the viewpoint of the referent. Both language and the speaker of language are negations of things: ". . . c'est la relation de l'homme aux choses que l'homme a décrite en décrivant le signe négativement. Il a décrit sa non-possession des choses, sa non-identification avec les choses. Il a décrit non seulement une négativité, mais une angoisse" (Meschonnic 1975:24-25). The subject, negation personified, suffers because of the negation. And the only end to this peculiarly semiotic kind of suffering is the cessation of all signifying behavior, i.e., death. In the meantime the subject continues to suffer, continues to signify.

If we can grant that there is an at least vaguely painful absence associated with semiosis, then we have granted that the psychology of *affect* is relevant to semiotics. No sign is an island, but is attached to affects of various kinds, and it is the business of psychology to study affects, however possible it may be to reduce the affects themselves to signs. If the signifying subject feels an affect such as pain at the absence of what is signified, then both the psychologist and the semiotician should have something to say about the semiosis. When a child whines, for example, the semiotician can tell us that the linguistic feature [+nasal] is adding emphasis to the utterance, is behaving like certain suprasegmental features would in an adult utterance. The psychoanalyst would be able to add, however, that the [+nasal] feature is associated wtih an archaic anxiety about the absence of the mother's breast, for nasalization (occlusion of the oral cavity) is precisely what happens when the child vocalizes while nursing at the breast (see Jakobson 1960b).

Sign and affect become especially inseparable in poetic discourse. It is not enough to say that poetry draws special attention toward the sign without also saying that special attention is drawn toward the affect(s) attached to the sign. Thus when Jakobson tells us that the poetic function is "the set (Einstellung[1]) toward the MESSAGE as such" (1960a:356), we are obliged to add a psychoanalytic perspective: the poetic function is also a set toward the absence of what the message signifies. That is, whenever the speaking subject waxes poetic, we have to suspect an aggravated absence. Putting the linguistic and psychoanalytic perspectives together, we may define the poetic function of language as *simultaneous sets toward the presence of the message and the absence of what the message signifies*. The poetic function of language attracts our attention not only toward language as such, but also toward the absence of something which never was and never can be within mere language. Poetry is an especially efficient vehicle for signifying things that *have* to be absent, such as prohibited or physically impossible acts. A lyric poet will not, for example, be very likely to commit incest with his sister, but he can signify the incest if he has the wherewithal to construct an adequately defensive complex of signs that presents the incestuous fantasy in disguise. Or an epic poet, though he can never in reality be omniscient or omnipotent, can at least signify his fantasy of omniscience and omnipotence by inventing an omniscient narrator and a hero of many exploits. External reality need not be tested by either the creator or the receiver of the poem because the very absence of external reality is implicit in the poetic function. But internal reality — fantasies, fears, desires, etc. — remains as present as the language which signifies it. When the poet has finally mastered the arrangement of signifiers, internal reality is made present to us, but the poet can always beg off if external reality seems to compromise internal reality in the slightest:

> . . . there is this consolation:
> If it turns out to be not worth doing, I haven't done it;
> If the sight appalls me, I have seen nothing;
> If the victory is pyrrhic, I haven't won it.
> And so from a day replete with rumors
> Of things being done on the other side of the mountains
> A nucleus remains, a still-perfect possibility
> That can be kept indefinitely.
>
> (John Ashbery, *Grand Galop*)

NOTE

[1] The basic treatise on the psychological notion of set (Russian *ustanovka*) is Uznadze 1966.

II

Automorphic Structures in the Poem's Grammatical Space

The analysis of poetry always presupposes spatialization of the temporal (dynamic, unidimensional, unidirectional) discourse. This spatialization has been expressed in various guises. Blanchot speaks of "l'espace du poème" and "l'espace littéraire" (1955:146). Derrida discusses the critic's "métaphore géometrique" (1967a:35). Lotman dwells on the "problema xudožestvennogo prostranstva" ("problem of artistic space") and even utilizes Lobačevskij's non-Euclidean geometry as a model for the literary work (1971:265-79, 257-58). Jakobson frequently observes the numerous spatial analogies between verbal and visual art (1961:408-10; 1970a:3-23; 1971a:3-4). Poeticists have simply grown accustomed to 'looking at' the poem, as if it really were that object which the poet writes down in a plane.

The spatial analogy is indispensable, but it *is* nevertheless an analogy. The very notion of analogy has been given the existential lie by Lacan (1966:889-92). And Eco observes (1972:8) that analogies are "vague and ineffable" by nature. In short, the notion of ἀναλογία itself cannot be non-tautologously defined and belongs entirely within the realm of Kantian pure intuition. True, the psychologist might succeed in reducing the spatial analogy to synesthesia or to some sort of identity in the conditions of perception. Or, to take another step in the reductionistic direction, the neuropsychologist (following Luria's exploratory research) might find that the spatial analogy depends on the simultaneous or 'quasi-spatial' neural syntheses that occur in the occipito-parietal cortex.[1] But there will always be a crucial epistemological limitation: the cerebral cortex itself is ultimately the only instrument we have for understanding the cerebral cortex.

Aware of the possible "coupures épistémologiques" in the spatial analogy, we may nonetheless explore some of the interesting consequences of the analogy. To begin with, there are two fundamental ways in which the analogy is applied to a poem: 1) the *grammatical structure* of a poem is spatialized as, for example, when Jakobson speaks of the "manifestly spatial" arrangement of animate and inanimate nouns in a poem by Blake (1970a:6), or when he speaks of "positionally corresponding entities" in a poem's syntactic organization (1966a:399); 2) the *semantic content* may require that the addressee visualize or imagine a space containing various object-configurations ("images", "pictures"). The present essay concentrates on the first of these two kinds of spatialization. The two need not, of course, be unrelated. For example, a poem by Afanasij Fet begins with the distich

(1)   Mesjac zekral'nyj plyvët po lazurnoj pustyne,
      Travy stepnye unizany vlagoj večernej . . . ,

and ends epanaleptically, but with a mirror reversal:

(2)   Travy stepnye sverkajut rosoju večernej,
      Mesjac zekral'nyj bežit po lazurnoj pustyne.

This mirroring is a particularly appropriate syntagmatic *icon* (Peirce's term) for the twice-occurring visual image of a mirror-like moon. That is, a similarity (expressible as 'mirrorness') between an arrangement in the analogical grammatical space and an object in the visual space conjured up by the poem establishes a semiotic link between the two spaces.

The advice of the mathematician Hermann Weyl provides a good starting point for investigating the structures in a poem's grammatical space:

Whenever you have to do with a structure-endowed entity Σ try to determine its group of automorphisms, the group of all those element-wise transformations which leave all structural relations undisturbed. You can expect to gain a deep insight into the constitution of Σ in this way. (1952:144)

An automorphism, in the strictly geometrical sense, is a transformation which carries a figure into another figure that is indiscernible from the first if each of the two figures is considered by itself, i.e., an automorphism is a transformation which carries a figure into itself.[2]

For example, the reflection of an object in a plane is an automorphism. Left is the automorphism of right. Congruent triangles are automorphic to one another.

If Σ is a poem, some of the unconsciously assumed automorphic relationships in its grammatical space are as follows:

... one syllable is equalized with any other syllable of the same sequence; word stress is assumed to equal word stress, as unstress equals unstress; prosodic long is matched with long, and short with short; word boundary equals word boundary, no boundary equals no boundary; syntactic pause equals syntactic pause, no pause equals no pause. (Jakobson 1960a:358)

Superimposed upon these basic automorphisms in the poetic discourse are others, more complex and varied. But certain *a priori* considerations require that, no matter how intricate the automorphic structures become, they can always be reduced to no more than four types. That is, if one utilizes a two-dimensional analogue for the poem's grammatical space,[3] and if one admits the two oppositional variables *polarity* and *sequence* as characteristic of the space, then the following configurations become possible:

SYMMETRIES (no polar reversal)
(3) PROPER CONGRUENCE OR PARALLELISM (neither polar nor sequential reversal)
$[\alpha P]_1, [\alpha P]_2, \ldots [\alpha P]_n \rightarrow [\alpha P]_1, [\alpha P]_2, \ldots [\alpha P]_n$
(4) REFLEXIVE CONGRUENCE OR MIRROR SYMMETRY (only sequential reversal)
$[\alpha P]_1, [\alpha P]_2, \ldots [\alpha P]_n \rightarrow [\alpha P]_n, \ldots [\alpha P]_2, [\alpha P]_1$
ANTISYMMETRIES (polar reversal)
(5) PROPER ANTI-CONGRUENCE (only polar reversal)
$[\alpha P]_1, [\alpha P]_2, \ldots [\alpha P]_n \rightarrow [-\alpha P]_1, [-\alpha P]_2, \ldots [-\alpha P]_n$
(6) REFLEXIVE ANTI-CONGRUENCE (both polar and sequential reversal)
$[\alpha P]_1, [\alpha P]_2, \ldots [\alpha P]_n \rightarrow [-\alpha P]_n, \ldots [-\alpha P]_2, [-\alpha P]_1$

The subscripts are sequence indicators, α is a sign that is consistently plus or consistently minus, and P is a phonological, morphological, or syntactic property[4] (or bundle of properties). These four mappings formalize something which previous investigators have discussed in less formal fashion. The labels for the mappings represent an attempt to synthesize the terminology used on different occasions by Weyl, Šubnikov, and Jakobson.[5]

Some terminological and perceptual problems arise in regard to the polar variable. For example:

(7) $+ + \rightarrow + +$,
(8) $+ + - - \rightarrow + + - -$.

Application of Occam's razor will rule out the terms reflexive congruence and reflexive anti-congruence, respectively, for these configurations: a proper congruence is the simplest designation for both. Occasionally, however, Occam's razor is not sharp enough, as in

(9) $+ - \rightarrow - +$,
(10) $+ - + - \rightarrow - + - +$,

where either polarity or sequence (but not both) may be taken as the variable at work. Ordinarily sequence is the first variable to come to mind in such cases, as when Jakobson (1966a:412-13) terms the automorphic configuration in "/pojaɣ́laṣ gɾ́ɪvna/" (from a Russian folk song) a reflexive congruence, rather than viewing it as an anti-symmetry. In other words, Jakobson seems to be perceiving a sequential change in partially specified phonemes,

$$
(11) \quad / \quad \begin{matrix} P_1 & P_2 \\ V & I \end{matrix} \quad / \quad \rightarrow \quad / \quad \begin{matrix} P_2 & P_1 \\ I & V \end{matrix} \quad /,
$$

rather than a polar change in certain distinctive features,

(12)

$$
\begin{matrix} P_1 \\ \begin{bmatrix} -\text{vocalic} \\ +\text{consonantal} \\ +\text{grave} \\ \text{etc.} \end{bmatrix} \end{matrix}
\begin{matrix} P_2 \\ \begin{bmatrix} +\text{vocalic} \\ -\text{consonantal} \\ -\text{grave} \\ \text{etc.} \end{bmatrix} \end{matrix}
\rightarrow
\begin{matrix} P_1 \\ \begin{bmatrix} +\text{vocalic} \\ -\text{consonantal} \\ -\text{grave} \\ \text{etc.} \end{bmatrix} \end{matrix}
\begin{matrix} P_2 \\ \begin{bmatrix} -\text{vocalic} \\ +\text{consonantal} \\ +\text{grave} \\ \text{etc.} \end{bmatrix} \end{matrix}
$$

— despite the logical equivalence of the two mappings which describe the change. Thus the terminological problem cannot be solved without reference to perceptual operations in the addressee. For some reason perception of the sequence takes precedence over perception of the polarity. A similar priority of sequence over polarity determines how the addressee will perceive the rhyme scheme of the following poem by Fet:

(13)   Snilsja bereg mne skalistyj,
       More spalo pod lunoju,
       Kak rebënok dremlet čistyj, –
       I, po nëm skol'zja s toboju,
       V dym prozračnyj i volnistyj
       Šli almaznoj my stezeju.

The simplest description of the automorphic arrangement of contextually opposed sounds [-ístyj] and [-óju] would be a single antisymmetrical mapping between two tercets:

(14) $+ - + \rightarrow - + -$.

Yet a native speaker does not sense this antisymmetry, despite its
simple descriptive elegance. Rather, he hears the regular back-and-
forth alternation between [-ístyj] and [-óju], and groups the lines
into properly congruent distichs:

(15) $+ - \rightarrow + - \rightarrow + -$.

A polar reversal is thus again avoided. In fact, it appears that the
term 'antisymmetry' is psychologically justified only when no opera-
tion *other* than a polar reversal will yield an automorphic structure.
For example, Jakobson finds that certain adjacent lines of Blok's
"Devuška pela" do form a sensible "antisymmetrical figure"
(Jakobson 1966b:388):

(16) $_6$ I luč sijal na belom pleče,
       $_7$ I každyj iz mraka smotrel i slušal . . .
       U|/ U / U / U U / |
       U|/ U U / U U / U /|U

With the disyllabic interictic intervals of Blok's stress-meter
(*"dol'niki"*) contextually opposed to the monosyllabic interictic
intervals, the only possible automorphic relationship between the
lines is antisymmetrical:

(17) $+ + - \rightarrow - - +$.

This tendency of the addressee to look for sequential sameness or
reversal before looking for polar reversal may be expressed in terms
of a familiar Jakobsonian dichotomy: the semantic *contiguity process*

required to conceive of an automorphism's sequential relationships takes priority over the *similarity process* required to conceive of an automorphism's polarity relationships (polar opposition being a species of similarity).[6] The psychological or neurological reasons for this tendency remain to be investigated.

If automorphic structures are consciously or (more likely) unconsciously sensed by the addressee, then the question of their *aesthetic function* arises: what do automorphic structures have to do with the aesthetic pleasure gained by the addressee?

Here it is helpful to introduce the notion of cathexis (Strachey's translation of Freud's "Besetzung"). Cathexis is the investment of an object, person, or event with mental energy or affect. If the addressee is in some way enjoying a poem's 'harmonies' or 'symmetries', we may say that he is cathecting the automorphic configurations in the poem. Each automorphic structure is providing him with a particular formula for cathectic shift. Thus, if the addressee cathects the ordering of noun-phrase constituents in the opening line of Yeats' "Into the Twilight,"

(18)   *Out-worn heart* in a *time out-worn,*
       Mod͜N   N͜Mod
         NP   NP

then a very systematic (i.e., automorphic) cathectic shift is required to go over from the first configuration to the reflexively congruent second configuration. The same thing may be said of the line's reflexively congruent prosodic pattern:

(19)   / ∪ / ∪ → ∪ / ∪ /

And finally, the proper congruence of the two ends of the line (a lexical epanalepsis) adds further automorphicity to the cathectic shifts involved in perceiving the line.

Ernst Kris states that "the shifts in cathexis of mental energy which the work of art elicits are, we believe, pleasurable in themselves".[7] The automorphic structures of a work of art, however, not only engender shifts in cathexis, but assure that these shifts will be highly systematic. It is the very automorphicity of the cathectic shifts which is responsible for a large part of the pleasure gained by the addressee. Compare Edgar Allan Poe's description of the pleasure gained in the perception of "equality":

... man derives enjoyment from his perception of equality. Let us examine a crystal. We are at once interested by the equality between the sides and between the angles of one of its faces: the equality of the sides pleases us; that of the angles doubles the pleasure. On bringing to view a second face in all respects similar to the first, this pleasure seems to be squared; on bringing to view a third it appears to be cubed, and so on. (Poe 1904[1843]:16)

Poe is here describing, in his somewhat hyperbolic manner, the automorphic cathectic shifts that are elicited by a crystal rotated before the eyes. Of course Poe does not speak in terms of 'automorphisms'. But the lines, angles, and polygonal surfaces of a crystal do quite literally enter into automorphic relationships, and Poe shows an awareness of these relationships through use of the epithets "equal" and "in all respects similar". For Poe, the spatial analogy applies insofar as hearing the "equalities" of a poem in time is equivalent to seeing the "equalities" of a crystal in space. When one recognizes that the systematic cathectic shifts engendered by a crystal's automorphic structures in real space are functionally identical to those engendered by a poem's automorphic structures in grammatical space, one begins to appreciate the unconscious insight shown by Solov'ëv, for example, when he spoke of the "diamonds of Puškin, the pearls of Tjutčev, the emeralds and rubies of Fet . . ." (Radlov I:226).

We might ask, however, why automorphic cathectic shifts should have any more hedonistic potential than non-automorphic ones. The psychoanalyst would answer: automorphic cathectic shifts are more 'economical', that is, they involve less psychic expenditure. The repetition of linguistic elements which necessarily occurs in an automorphic pattern provides the addressee with something familiar, something already 'used', and therefore something 'cheaper'. Freud says that the ". . . rediscovery of what is familiar is pleasurable, and . . . it is not difficult for us to recognize this pleasure as a pleasure in economy and to relate it to economy in psychical expenditure" ("Jokes and Their Relation to the Unconscious," 1960 [1905] VIII:120). He adds that ". . . rhymes, alliterations, refrains, and other forms of repeating verbal sounds which occur in verse, make use of the same source of pleasure – the rediscovery of something familiar" (ibid. 122).[8]

This "economy" explanation of the pleasure yielded by automorphic devices seems incontestable enough. Yet it is well known that the unfamiliar or the unexpected in poetry can also be gratifying, which is to say that an "uneconomy" of psychic expenditure can also be involved in the yield of aesthetic pleasure. But there is usually a good psychological reason for violating an expected automorphic pattern. For example, Shakespeare violates the train of metrical automorphisms (specifically, iambs) by introducing two hypermetrical stresses in the last of the following lines from *Midsummer-Night's Dream* (I, 1, 134):

(20)   Ay me! for aught that ever I could read,
       Could ever hear by tale or history,
       The course of true *love* never did *run* smooth . . .

This sensible break in the iambic pattern definitely frustrates metrical expectations. But note that at the same time it offers an iconic commentary (cf. (1)-(2), above) on the overt semantics of the line (metrically, the line is saying: "the course of iambic pentameter never did run smooth either"). The metrical break is therefore appropriate or 'motivated' and is bound to yield pleasure to the sensitive reader. The pleasure is even an 'economy' pleasure insofar as any pun (here a metrical pun) economizes on psychic expenditure by 'short-circuiting' two layers of meaning in one phonetic representation (cf. Freud VIII:119-20). Whether or not the 'economy' of the metrical pun compensates for the 'uneconomy' of frustrated metrical expectation cannot easily be determined, if only because no method of quantifying psychic expenditure exists. And still further complexity is added to the problem when the addressee is conditioned to expect a *non*-automorphic component in a position where an automorphic component actually occurs. Thus, certain kinds of deviation from the ideal pattern of metrical automorphisms are in fact so common as to themselves become automatized or expected. For example, the law of regressive accentual dissimilation in Russian binary meters dictates that the penultimate ictus is very frequently unfulfilled (Taranovski 1953; Bailey 1968), which is to say that the penultimate foot will not actually be automorphic to the immediately preceding foot in a predictably large percentage of cases.

Incidentally, the term 'foot' is used advisedly here. The dismissal of this automorphic component in the Halle-Keyser theory of metrics (1971:167) simply contradicts the psychological evidence. Tests in the perception of rhythm have always indicated that the *subjective experiencing of groups* is an essential factor.[9] The French experimental psychologist Paul Fraisse found that even when a regularly periodic series of absolutely identical stimuli is presented to the subject, the stimuli are always segregated or grouped into units of two, three or four (1956:9). For Fraisse, ". . . grouping is the result of a comprehensive and, as it were, simultaneous apprehension of several elements which form one unit of perception" (1963:72). Such a psychological operation has all the characteristics of what Luria terms the "simultaneous" or "quasi-spatial" syntheses (see note 1), and is a perfect illustration of Lashley's statement that "the temporal sequence is readily translated into a spatial concept" (1961:192).

In many cases the train of metrical automorphisms exists in the poet's mind even before a conscious semantic content is fitted to the train. Andrej Voznesenskij, for example, begins a poem in the following manner: "I may be walking down the street or in the woods — perhaps I'm strolling through Rome — and a rhythm starts inside, maybe connected with my breathing, fast or slow" (Voznesensky-Kunitz 1972:38). Compare Paul Valéry:

As I was following the street where I live, I was suddenly *seized* [*saisi*] by a rhythm which imposed itself on me and which soon impressed me with its strange functioning . . . . Another rhythm then came to double the first and to combine with it . . . . (1959 [1937] :1322)

Eventually, Valéry says, the ". . . composition became more and more complicated and soon exceeded in its complexity anything which I could reasonably produce with my usual rhythmic faculties" (*ibid.*). The American psychoanalyst A. A. Brill found out that, in one of his manic-depressive patients who wrote and published poetry, the repetition of rhythmical groups containing nonsense syllables (e.g., "he hem, he hem, dem dem, nem, nem, he hem, he hem," etc.) would go on for several days before an actual poem emerged (1931:368). Note the compulsive character of the metrical rhythm in all of these examples. The poet to a greater or lesser degree loses conscious control of the production of metrical automorphisms.

The addressee of a poem is hardly insensitive to the repetition compulsion ("Wiederholungszwang," to use Freud's term[10]) which originally generates the train of metrical automorphisms. Children are especially prone to exaggerate the automorphicity of the metrical train by reciting poetry in an extremely sing-song fashion. Adults too cannot escape the sway of the metrical train. Thus, when a native speaker of Russian encountered the following line in her reading of Deržavin's "Pamjatnik" (1795),

(21) Slux *projdet* obo mne ot Belyx vod do Černyx,

she hesitated for an instant, then very deliberately pronounced [prójdet], knowing perfectly well that [prajdót] is the normal pronunciation. "Because of the meter" was her justification, which is to say that she must have felt a compulsion to repeat the iambic pattern of the two previous quatrains. This experiment, incidentally, was possible only because of a diachronic gap between the poet and the addressee: the literary Russian of Deržavin's day was still so influenced by Lomonosov's stylistic precepts as to allow such Slavonicisms as *prídet, pójdet, pójdem*, etc. (all prefix-stressed verbs of motion) rather than the colloquial Russian forms *pridét, pojdét, podjém*, etc.[11]

The compulsive quality of the metrical automorphisms distinguishes them from the other kinds of automorphisms in the grammatical space. Metrical automorphisms are also unique insofar as they pervade the *entire* poem: if a poem is metrical, then every single syllable participates in the poem's metrical structure, whereas not every single syllable of the poem participates in such other automorphic structures as rhyme, anaphora, syntactic parallelism, etc. It is this all-pervasive characteristic of the metrical automorphisms which gives them the power of metonymically representing a poem which the poet may not even have formulated yet. Finally, the pattern of metrical automorphisms sharply differs from other automorphic patterns in that it superimposes a system of coordinates upon the grammatical space and thereby serves to 'chart' that space. For example, when asked where a given constituent is 'located' in a poem, more often than not a *line* is specified. Conversely, when the addressee encounters an enjambement (run-on-line) in a poem, he becomes 'disoriented' or loses his 'bearings' in the grammatical space.

Carl Jung has investigated the psychological function of a type of symbol called the *mandala* (from the Sanscrit word meaning 'circle'). For the student of automorphic structures, the mandala is interesting because it is almost always designed in such a way as to include one or more mirror symmetries (reflexive congruences). In Figure 1, for example, a seven-year-old boy has explicitly introduced the vertical and horizontal axes of symmetry.

Mandalas are produced (drawn, painted, modelled, danced) as an instrument of meditation by various Hindu and Buddhist mystics. They also appear quite spontaneously in certain pathological psychic states:

As a rule a mandala occurs in conditions of psychic dissociation or disorientation, for instance in the case of children between the ages of eight and eleven whose parents are about to be divorced, or in adults who, as the result of a

Figure 1
(After Jung 1959, fig. 33)

neurosis and its treatment, are confronted with the problem of opposites in human nature and are consequently disoriented; or again in schizophrenics whose view of the world has become confused, owing to the invasion of incomprehensible contents from the unconscious. (Jung 1959:3)

The function of the mandala is restitutive. It helps the subject regain some control over his chaotic mental state. The construction of a mandala "... is evidently an *attempt at self-healing* on the part of

Nature, which does not spring from conscious reflection, but from an instinctive impulse" (*ibid.*, 4). Ultimately, Jung asserts, the mandala relates back to an original "archetype of wholeness" that is inherent in the human species. But the archetypal or diachronic aspects of the mandala need not detain us here. For our purposes, the question is: can Jung's synchronic interpretation of the mandalas which occur in real space aid us in interpreting the mandala-like constituents which sometimes occur in a poem's grammatical space?

Consider, for example, William Blake's octastich "Infant Sorrow:"

(22) My mother groand! my father wept.
Into the dangerous world I leapt:
Helpless, naked, piping loud:
Like a fiend hid in a cloud,

Struggling in my fathers hands:
Striving against my swaddling bands:
Bound and weary I thought best
To sulk upon my mothers breast.

In his detailed linguistic study of this poem, Roman Jakobson (1970a:3-11) finds an abundance of mirror symmetries. Most of them involve a division of the poem into *four* rhyming distichs (n.b., Jung consistently links the notion of "quaternity" to mandalas: 4, 15-16, 23, 36-38, 46, *et passim*). The frequency of verb forms in each distich, for instance, shows the following pattern:

(23) 3   2 → 2   3
    I   II   III   IV

The distribution of prepositions is likewise reflexively congruent:

(24) 1   2 → 2   1
    I   II   III IV

On the level of syntax, the 'inner' distichs are subordinated to the immediately contiguous lines of the 'outer' distichs, yielding the following mirror pattern of subordinated (S) and unsubordinated (U) distichs:

(25) U   S → S   U
    I   II   III   IV

A further mirror symmetry is described by Jakobson:

The opening words of the poem — $_1My$ *mother* — reappear once more at its end — $_8my$ *mothers* — and jointly with the subject *I* of the second and seventh lines, they display mirror symmetry. The first of these two pronouns is followed by the pair of semipredicates $_3Helpless$, *naked*, while the second *I* is preceded by a syntactically analogous pair: $_7Bound$ *and weary*. The placement and chiastic structure of this pair retain the principle of mirror symmetry. (1970a:8)

The accumulation of mirror symmetries in the poem's grammatical space leads Jakobson to draw an interesting parallel with the use of visual perspective: "in particular, the headwords, the principal clauses and the prominent motifs which fill the diverging outer couplets stand out against accessory and subordinate contents of the contiguous inner couplets, quite similar to the converging lines of a background in a pictorial perspective" (*ibid.*).

Jakobson's analogical interpretation of the grammatical space of Blake's poem comes remarkably close to describing a mandala. Structurally, the presence of mirror symmetries in Blake's poem and in a mandala is what justifies a comparison of the two.

If the mandala-like constituents in Blake's poem perform a restitutive or healing function (as Jung would argue), then the motivation or need for such a function is not far to find. The poem, after all, very explicitly describes the trauma of birth. The intense anxiety which accompanies an infant's leap "$_2$ Into the dangerous world" is frequently discussed in the psychoanalytic literature. For example, Otto Rank (1929 [1924]) claims that the intensity of the birth trauma determines whether or not the adult will later be able to control his anxiety states. For Freud, ". . . the act of birth is the first experience of anxiety, and thus the source and prototype of the affect of anxiety" ("Interpretation of Dreams," 1953 [1909], V, 400-01).[12]

By means of his poem Blake recaptures the condition of "psychic dissociation and disorientation" (Jung) connected with the act of birth. In other words, the overt semantic content of the poem is Blake's way of fulfilling a compulsion to repeat the traumatic and anxiety-ridden birth scene. The poem's mandala-like constituents, on the other hand, help to counteract the disorienting and painful anxiety of the scene. They aid in restoring the poet's psychic equanimity even as this equanimity is being shaken by the compulsive act. Thematically, the restitutive function of the mandala-like structures is reflected in the child's climactic restoration of union with its mother: "$_7$ . . . I thought best / $_8$ To sulk upon my mothers breast."

Needless to say, the sensitive addressee who is 'resonating' with Blake's regressive fantasy also experiences both the psychic disturbance and the mandala-like antidote to the disturbance.

It cannot of course be claimed that every single mirror symmetry in a poem's grammatical space performs the function which Jung attributes to mandalas (e.g., the mirror symmetry in (1)-(2), above, seems to function primarily as an icon for the mirror-like moon). But when a poem's entire grammatical space is permeated with numerous mirror symmetries, then their possible therapeutic function has to be taken into serious consideration.

Here it may be objected that *all* the linguistic structures in a poem, automorphic and non-automorphic, perform a restitutive or therapeutic function of some sort, and that the mirror symmetries are therefore not at all unique in their function. Such an objection would seem to follow from Holland's cogent thesis (1968:130-31) that the linguistic structure as a whole (= form) acts as a defense mechanism to help protect the ego against any potentially dangerous and regressive fantasy elicited by the poem.[13] But an *accumulation* of mirror symmetries about a single axis of symmetry is therapeutic in a unique way. Not only do these symmetries defensively distract the subject's attention away from a possibly ego-distonic fantasy and toward themselves, as do all of the poem's linguistic devices, but they also mimic the subject's entrance into and exit from that regressed state required to apprehend the poem's underlying fantasy. That is, just as the subject *returns* (by the end of the poem) from his regressed position in the unconscious to his initial unregressed position, so too the mirror symmetries *return* the subject from the central position of the grammatical space to a position that is equivalent to (automorphic to) the initial position. The parallel between Freud's topography of the psychic apparatus ("die Topik") and the topography of the grammatical space is here inescapable. The well-known topographical regression to and progression from a point in the unconscious ("ein anderer Schauplatz") where the fantasy is enacted receives a palpable icon in the topographical movement toward and retreat from a single axis of several mirror symmetries. In the case of Blake's "Infant Sorrow", the affective strength of this iconic bond is so great that it seems artificial to disentangle the comfortable feeling of return or completion engendered by the poem's mirror symmetries from the comforting feeling of having 'pulled out' of the regressive birth fantasy. In other words, the mirror symmetries are not only iconically *signifying* the psychological regression/progression, they are *facilitating* it as well. Clearly, the semiotic and psychoanalytic considerations are here inseparable. At the same time, the Jungian interpretation (above) of the mandala-like structures in the poem is translated into explicitly Freudian terms.

The present analysis of automorphic structures in the poem's grammatical space concentrates on symmetries because 1) not all grammatical properties involve a binary opposition in sign (see note 4), and 2) even the formally potential antisymmetries are, whenever possible, perceived as symmetries. The functional role of a poem's automorphic structures is quite varied. Automorphic structures may 1) iconically signify and facilitate the subject's own internal topo-graphical regression/progression (mandala-like automorphisms); 2) participate in the overall linguistic structure's defensive distraction of attention away from any ego-distonic fantasy; 3) 'chart' the gram-matical space (metrical automorphisms); 4) provide an outlet for the compulsion to repeat; 5) become involved in the 'economy' and 'un-economy' of psychic expenditure required to perceive the poem; 6) serve as a medium for highly systematic cathectic shifts; and 7) iconically signify certain elements in the semantic content. This functional variety of the automorphic structures gives them a promi-nent place among the other grammatical structures in a poem.

NOTES

[1] Lesions to the occipito-parietal cortex involve "... disturbance of synthesis of individual elements into simultaneous (usually spatial) groups ... leaving intact the synthesis of elements organized serially in time." See Luria 1966b:102.
[2] See Weyl 1952:18. For a more mathematically detailed treatment of auto-morphisms, see Weyl 1949:72-84, and Lehner 1966.
[3] Spatial analogues which would give the poem's grammatical space three or more dimensions are certainly conceivable, but will not be explored in depth here. Three dimensional conceptions of the poem are hinted at by Poe (see below, p. 22), by Solov'ëv (see below, p. 22), and by Jakobson (see below, p. 28).
[4] If the property in question does not involve a binary opposition in sign (e.g., if it is a grammatical category such as noun, verb, adjective, etc.), then the sym-metries will be the only automorphic structures possible.
[5] Weyl's book (since it deals with symmetry, not antisymmetry) makes only some passing remarks on positive-negative relationships (1952:20, 25). Šubnikov gives numerous examples of figures related by polar opposition or "anti-equality": a drop of water in air vs. a bubble of air in water, a crystal vs. its "negative crystal" (the multi-faced liquid within the crystal), the growth pattern vs. the dissolution pattern of a crystal, a positron vs. an electron, a bolt vs. a nut, etc. Šubnikov recognizes the four possible automorphic relationships (though he does not use the term 'automorphism') that can exist between paired

configurations: "having accepted four kinds of equality [ravenstvo], we are likewise obliged to sanction four types of symmetrical transformations [preobraženija]: 1) motions [dviženija], 2) mirror-motions, 3) anti-motions [antidviženija] and 4) mirror-anti-motions, taking anti-motion to mean a motion accompanied by a change in sign of the figure, and taking mirror-anti-motion to mean a mirror-motion accompanied by a change in sign of the figure..." (Šubnikov 1951:7-8). Compare Jakobson's article on Chinese regulated verse, where he speaks of "... SYMMETRY PROPER as well as REFLEXIVE and ... ANTISYMMETRY which in turn proves to be either PROPER or REFLEXIVE." (Jakobson 1970a:602)

6   See Jakobson and Halle 1956:55-82 and Laferrière 1972:39-41.

7   See Kris 1952:63. Compare an earlier statement made by Freud: "when our psychic apparatus does not actually act in search of some urgently needed gratifications we let this apparatus itself work for pleasure gain. *We attempt to gain pleasure from its very activity.*" Quoted by Kris 315.

8   Freud cites Aristotle and the psychologist Karl Groos in discussing the 'economy principle'. He does not seem to be aware of the fact that the most outspoken exponent of the economy principle before him was Herbert Spencer (see 1875:9-27). He does, however, cite Spencer's "psychic damming" theory of laughter (Freud, 1960 [1905]:146). Curiously enough, Zipf's well-known "principle of least effort" does not take cognizance of Freud's "economy principle".

9   One of the many studies is Woodrow 1909. In this work the chapter entitled "The Meaning of Rhythmical Grouping" (53-62) is most relevant. A more recent experimental study is "Le groupement rythmique" in Fraisse 1956:9-22. See also Valentine 1962:233-34 and Chatman 1965:18-29. Some aspects of the pathology of the grouping phenomenon have also been studied in Luria 1966b: 343-48.

10 In his discussion of the repetition compulsion Freud does not mention stylistic or literary repetitions. See Freud, XVII, 238; XVIII, 14ff. Sacvan Bercovitch's study, however, places the repetition compulsion in a literary context: "... the same motives which impel writers to play recurrently upon certain themes and images may lead them to a corresponding stylistic repetition-compulsion. Grammar, vocabulary, syntax – the whole semantic-structural complex of language lends itself to an investigation of this kind." See Bercovitch 1968:614.

11 These instances are quoted from Lomonosov's literary practice:

No myšlju, *pridet* liš' godina,
                    (Second Ode, iambic tetrameter, 1741)

Vsevyšnij *pojdet* pred toboju,
                    (Eighth Ode, iambic tetrameter, 1746)

My *projdem* s nim skvoz' ogn' i vody.
                    (Eighth Ode, iambic tetrameter, 1746)

12 Freud did not entirely accept Rank's views on the later effects of the birth trauma. See: "Inhibition, Symptoms and Anxiety," 1959 (1926) XX:150-153.

13 Compare the following from Wordsworth's famous preface of 1849: "... there can be little doubt that more pathetic situations and sentiments, that is, those which have a greater proportion of pain connected with them, may be endured in metrical composition, especially in rhyme, than in prose" (quoted in Shands 1971:110).

III

Automorphic Structures, Information, and the Lifting of Repression

Information in the literary situation (creating a poem, reciting a poem, reading a poem, etc.) is conveyed by means of linguistic signs. The science which studies the quantity of information conveyed in literary and other semiotic situations is information theory. According to information theory, the more predictable the sequence of signs in a signifying system, the less information that can be conveyed. Conversely, the less predictable the sequence of signs, the more information that can be conveyed. This regularity is very much like the organization of particles in a closed thermodynamic system, where the more predictable (non-random) the behavior of the particles, the less so-called 'entropy' of the system, and vice-versa. Many information theoreticians in fact use the terms 'information' and 'entropy' interchangeably. A general statement of the information conveyed in a signifying system is given by the following (modification of the) Shannon-Weaver equation:

$$(1) \quad H = h_1 + h_2 - \beta.$$

where

$(2) \quad H =$ information conveyed (entropy or uncertainty in the system),

$h_1 =$ capacity for conveying meaningful messages (range of choices of messages),

$h_2 =$ capacity to convey the same message in different ways (synonymy, flexibility),

β = constraints that control possibilities of information transfer.

(See Shannon & Weaver 1949; Revzin 1962:289; Lotman 1971:38, Rewar 1976: 3-4)[1]

According to Kolmogorov and Revzin, variations specifically in the value of h_2 are the key to measuring poetic entropy or information. Languages which have a low value for flexibility (e.g., artificial languages which have no synonymy) will not be suited for poetry, while languages which have high flexibility are best suited for poetry. According to information theory the structural constraints which operate in poetry (such as those which I above termed automorphic structures) increase the value of β and therefore limit the value of H. That is, the information conveyed should decrease as β increases, because β is precisely that collection of elements which enhances the predictability of the sequence of signs.[2] Metrical structure, for example, is a kind of automorphic structure which makes the sequence more predictable. Thus to say

(3)   The curfew tolls the knell of parting day (Thomas Gray)

is to impose an iambic constraint which would *not* allow, say, a paraphrase by passivization:

(4)   *The knell of parting day is tolled by the curfew.

What the metrical constraint does is enhance the predictability of the line to the extent that certain kinds of variation upon the line are impossible. In effect, the increase in the value of β by the addition of an iambic rhythmic constraint decreases the value of h_2, the capacity of the system to convey the same message in different ways, with a resulting overall decrease in the value of H, the overall information conveyed.[3] β is thus in some sense opposed to h_2 insofar as the conveyance of "poetic information" (Lotman) is concerned. According to Kolmogorov (Lotman 1971:38) the value of β cannot equal or exceed the value of h_2 in poetry. That is, in a language where $\beta \geqslant h_2$, poetic creativity is impossible (Rewar 1976:4).

The fact is, however, that the imposition of structural constraints also *helps* to convey information (as Lotman himself seems to recognize). For example, the very imposition of an iambic constraint in Gray's poem opens up the possibility of conveying certain kinds of information that would have been non-transmissible without the constraint. Not that the constraint itself is necessarily information. Rather, the constraint at least *facilitates* the conveyance of certain kinds of information even as it hinders the conveyance of other kinds of information. For example, without an iambic rhythm the addressee would not be lulled into dropping his defenses against the thoughts of (= semantic elements concerned with) death which in most other contexts are repressed. The notion of death is repeated time and again in Gray's rhythmicized discourse:

(5) Each in his narrow cell for ever laid,
     The rude forefathers of the hamlet *sleep*.

     The paths of glory lead but to the *grave* . . .

     Can Honour's voice provoke the silent dust,
     Or Flattery soothe the dull cold ear of *Death*?

     And many a holy text around she strews,
     That teach the rustic moralist to *die*.

     etc., etc.

We do not feel that the poet is harping on death, we do not resist the *conveyance of information about death* because the iambic rhythm, along with other automorphic structures (alternating rhyme, syntactic symmetries, etc.) and non-automorphic structures is keeping us in the proper 'mood' for the acceptance of such information (see above comments on poetic structures as defensive devices, p. 29; cf. also my discussion of metrical defense – Laferrière 1978a).[4] Thus, contrary to the exploratory proposals made by Kolmogorov, an increase in the value of β at the expense of the value of h_2 can actually help to convey information. Components in β can in fact have the effect of clearing the channel to promote the freer flow of information.

Some of the components included in β may carry information directly (become 'semanticized'), as when an automorphic structure occurs in a context that makes it an icon:

(6) Serdce b'etsja rovno, merno . . .,

                                                    (Anna Axmatova)

where the absolutely perfect trochaic rhythm (all ictuses fulfilled) and the perfect correspondence of word boundaries with foot boundaries strikingly suggests what the poet is talking about, namely, the perfectly regular rhythm of heartbeat. At other times a component of β may help to convey a meaning through synaesthesia, as when an alliterative accumulation of the 'liquid consonant' /l/ facilitates the signification of the notion of a flowing *liquid*:

(7)   Avec le doigt fané presseras-tu le sein
      Par qui coule en blancheur sibylline la femme . . .
                    (Mallarmé, as quoted by Fónagy 1970:107)

Or, to take another example, Puškin's masterful use of the bilabial phonemes /b/ and /p/ onomatopoetically helps convey the notion of popping champagne bottles:

(8)   Šipen'e penistyx bokalov
      I punša plamen' goluboj . . . .

Actually, in instances such as these it is not always clear whether we are dealing with onomatopoeia, synaesthesia, or iconicity, or some combination of all three (the terminological problems will certainly have to be worked out by psychologists and semioticians working together). But it is clear that such standard poetic devices, if they do not actually convey information, at least considerably facilitate the flow of information.

Whatever the constraints contributing to β may be, they are not gratuitous, they are not without informational consequences. Let us then modify equation (1) to read

(9) $H = h_1 + h_2 - (\beta_1 - \beta_2),$

where old $\beta = \beta_1 - \beta_2$; β_1 includes constraints that restrict information transfer; β_2 includes constraints that facilitate information transfer (some of the constraints may do both simultaneously, but to different kinds of information — such a situation requires a theory of information that will deal with quality as well as quantity of information).[5] Let me add that this new equation is only intended as a quasi-mathematical statement, and may well have to be modified in a more strictly mathematical study.

The increased information transfer resulting from the presence of automorphic and non-automorphic constraints is often connected with the psychological process of *deautomatization*. In fact the connection is causal. What a deautomatizing device (e.g., a sudden non-metrical syllable) does is cause the receiver to re-evaluate or re-perceive a segment of the text all over again, thereby enhancing the possibility that information that was not conveyed before the de-automatization be conveyed after or during the deautomatization process. Deautomatisation (or its aliases *ostranenie, aktualisace*, 'foregrounding', 'defamiliarization', etc.) is not itself the conveyance of information, but one of the *psychological conditions* which en-hances information flow, or signification. Clearly, there is no disentangling the psychological, informational, and semiotic aspects of this question. Those formalist, structuralist, and other theorists who make such a point of avoiding any 'psychologism' ("Psycho-logismus") fail to see the major psychological construct already embedded in their assumptions (for a more detailed discussion of automatization/deautomatization, see my paper on the familiarity/strangeness paradox, 1976a).

Information theoreticians have already made a connection be-tween the notion of information and notions of 'originality' or 'unexpectedness'. Such theoreticians quite literally treat information as a measure of originality:

To measure the *a priori* originality of a situation, the only procedure offered us by logic is to reckon its improbability. If a given message or event is certain, it teaches the receptor nothing and cannot modify his behavior. An unexpected event has by definition a zero probability; hence it substantially modifies the behavior of the receptor. This is the essential, well-established point of every study of behavior. On it one may build.

Hence we shall say information or originality is a function of the improba-bility of the received message. (Moles 1966:22)

This kind of 'improbability' or 'unexpectedness', however, does not always deautomatize the receiver's perceptual processes. For example, a statistically improbable (relatively unlikely) occurrence of the letter *w* in a passage of written French will hardly cause a psycho-logical deautomatization. We cannot rely on information theory to provide a precise mathematical description of what takes place during deautomatization, or at least we cannot count on information theory to predict when a given instance of deautomatization will take place. We can say that, whereas deautomatization facilitates information flow, the flow of information does not always result in deautomatization.

Let us return to the informational consequences of components included in β. It appears that, not only is the information not primarily a function of h_2, but that h_2 plays a rather minimal role altogether, i.e., $h_2 \rightarrow 0$. Conversely, it seems that the role of β has been underestimated, that β_2 in particular approaches or exceeds β_1. Compare a slice of poetic text with any one of the numerous possible paraphrases of the slice:

(10)   April is the cruellest month, breeding
        Lilacs out of the dead land, mixing
        Memory and desire, stirring
        Dull roots with spring rain.
                (T. S. Eliot, first quatrain of "The Burial of the
                Dead" in *The Waste Land*)

versus

(11)   April is the cruellest month and breeds
        Lilacs out of the dead land, mixes
        Memory and desire, stirrs
        Dull roots with spring rain.

(12)   Breeding lilacs out of the dead land,
        Mixing memory and desire,
        Stirring dull roots with spring rain,
        April is the cruellest month.

(13)   One of the cruellest months of the year is April,
        When lilacs grow from the cold earth, when
        Memory and desire get mixed together, and when
        Spring rain stirrs last year's dull roots.
        etc., etc.

No sensitive reader would claim that paraphrases (11)-(13) are as 'successful' or 'beautiful' as the original (10). From the viewpoint of information theory, (10) conveys more "poetic information" (Lotman) or "esthetic information" (Moles). The poet *could* have written any of the paraphrases (11)-(13), but in fact he did not. The paraphrases are inferior in their ability to carry information. The poet rejects his rough drafts and the reader rejects paraphrases because only one (or an extremely small set of very slight deviants from that one) text carries the desired information — which is not to say that the desired information has a narrow range of meaning, for the precision of the 'wording' is just what is needed to promote polysemy (what Empson terms "ambiguity"). The range of flexibility. h_2, may be great *before* the poet starts to signify his fantasy (e.g., there are many ways to deal with death besides the system of signifiers known as *The Burial of the Dead*), but once the poet begins to produce signifiers, his range of choices contracts enormously. Indeed, in retrospect, he feels that he had *no* choice (recall Tolstoj's remark to the effect that there would be no way to retell *Anna Karenina* except to write *Anna Karenina* all over again – which is in curious contrast to the work of many literary critics, who tend to claim that, if they had it to do all over again, they would do it differently). If the paraphrase is a questionable criterion in linguistics, it becomes even more questionable in literary theory, where paraphrase destroys so much information.[6] Consider the particularly clear example of (12), where mere reversal of the lines (which does not change the pattern of syntactic subordination) nonetheless spoils the quatrain. In the original (10) the month of April is personified right from the start by the epithet "cruellest", and the personification is continued and reinforced by a syntactically parallel sequence of participles that are capable of taking animate subjects ("breeding", "mixing", "stirring"). In (12), however, the parallelism is too obvious and does not perform any personifying function at all, at least not until the fourth line is reached, i.e., only retrospectively, only after we have reacted negatively to the obtrusiveness of the parallelism (we have a similar negative reaction to a rhythm that is too sing-song, unless it is performing a *signifying* function, as in (6) above). The arrangement of the participial clauses in (12) thus *interferes* with the conveyance of information about personification, whereas the arrangement in the original (10) *facilitates* the conveyance of such information (in information theoretical terms the 'bit' of information concerns a choice between the features [+human] and [−human]). Moreover, if we examine the word "cruellest" a little more carefully, we can see another reason why (12) is an inferior variant on the original. When reading the original, the personification in "cruellest" causes a slight deautomatization, i.e., causes us to reconsider the message and to wonder just what it means for a *month* to be "cruel". And no sooner do we wonder about this than Eliot provides an answer with the succeeding participial clause – the month is cruel because it *breeds* flowers from the *dead* land. That is, the cruelty is constituted by something vaguely sexual, and that has to do with death. But cruelty, sexuality, and death add up to a clear suggestion of sadistic sexuality, so that the personification of the month of April leads to a more specific characterization of just what kind of 'person' this month is, i.e., leads to the description of a sadistic personality. In effect, we can expect the burial of the dead to take place in April, the cruellest month (paronomastically related phonemes /r. . .il/ are in italics). In (12) this suggestion of sadistic sexuality is much weaker because "cruellest" is separated from "breeding" by two intervening lines. We are forced to consider only in retrospect just what "cruellest" means, rather than being spoon fed with an instant definition in "breeding". Besides, the poem must go on, which is to say that there would not be enough time to absorb the implications of "cruellest" when listening to (12) as opposed to listening to the original. In sum, there are all kinds of hinderences to the transfer of significant information in the paraphrase of the original. What in ordinary speech is an optional ordering of participial phrases becomes in Eliot's original quatrain a mandatory (albeit ad hoc) formal constraint, a component in β that facilitates information transfer.[7]

If paraphrases of poetry destroy poetry, or if, as Robert Frost said, poetry is what is lost in the translation, then whatever constraints are operating in the original must therefore be mandatory to the conveyance of whatever 'poetry' is in the original. The fact that the constraints do not tolerate deviation does not by any means imply, however, that the constraints are all alike. Indeed, the immense variety of constraints available to the poet is precisely what makes poetry 'creative' − cf. the Greek verb ποιέω, 'to make, create'. If ordinary language is creative, as Chomsky often asserts, poetry is all the more so because the poet has at his disposal not only the latitude permitted him by ordinary language, but also the right ('license' in classical literary theory, 'choice' in information theory) to deviate from the constraints of everyday language. Thus a constraint such as "place the pronoun before the preposition in a prepositional phrase" in such lines as

(14)   me under a opens,
(15)   me up at does   (e.e. cummings)

does deviate noticeably from constraints in standard English (see Fairley 1975:93). Or, the constraints can vary in the extent of their application. That is, they may be limited to the one poem in which they appear, or they may be so widespread as to characterize a whole period of literary history or a whole genre. Thus many of the peculiar syntactic constraints in cummings are very 'local', while a constraint such as the proscription against fulfillment of an ictus by the stressed syllable of a polysyllabic word characterized almost all the verse written by nineteenth century Russian poets.

The variety of constraints, then, is great. But once applied, they are inflexible. Successful verbal art does not tolerate paraphrase. In particular the 'greatest' or 'most beautiful' literary art does not tolerate deviance from the constraints.[8] If we memorize a passage from Puškin, for example, we are obliged to memorize it *exactly*, otherwise it will sound like a rough draft or like a passage from some minor poet in the Puškin pleiad.

Although the poet has his 'poetic license', there is no corresponding 'reader's license' to change what the poet has established. But even the poet exercises his license only because he *has* to in order to convey certain items of information. The poet is 'driven' or 'inspired' by information that, in psychoanalytic terms, is usually repressed in everyday language. The poet's freedom or license is thus illusory, is only an artifact constructed by the critics who cannot consciously perceive the purposive or end-directed nature of the linguistic deviations practiced by the poet. Here the psychoanalytic principle of psychical determinism (e.g., *SE* XV:106-09), i.e., the notion that certain kinds of signifying practices are *determined* by repressed semantic material negates the information theoretical concept of 'choice'. The fact is that the poet has little choice. The poet does what he has to do, as anyone who has ever felt the spontaneous need to write poetry knows. The only freedom the poet asks for, paradoxically, is the freedom to do what he has to do. For example, the poet asks his editors not to tamper with the supposed 'liberties' he has taken with language (or with literary norms, or with political norms). Thus in opposition to the rather superficial idea of the poet as 'creator' we have the stark reality of the poet as an organism determined and driven by unconscious forces. The old scholastic debate of free will vs. determinism resolves itself in the poetic context as the poet's *choice* to be *determined* by signs emerging from his unconscious. The non-poet, on the other hand, is precisely the kind of subject who does *not* choose to be determined by such signs.

Although there is a conflict between the information theoretical concept of choice and the psychoanalytic principle of psychical determinism, not all aspects of information theory and psychoanalysis need to clash. Let us raise the following question: how can the psychoanalytic interpretation of automorphic structures proposed above (Ch. II) be related to the information theoretical interpretation of components (a great many of them automorphic structures) constituting β? At this point it is impossible to answer such a question with anything like mathematical precision. But I would like to propose the following hypothesis which may at some time in the future be testable by more sophisticated methods than we now have available.

Let us assume that the cathexis or neural excitation[9] involved in the perception and processing of language decreases when automorphic structures are present (see the above claim that automorphic structures provide an 'economy' of psychical expenditure). If, however, the presence of automorphisms 'economizes' on cathexis, then we must ask what happens to the 'saved' or 'left-over' cathexis. The answer must have something to do with the fact that we have just established, namely, that an increase in the value of β by the presence of automorphic structures *facilitates* the conveyance of information. Specifically, the 'saved' cathexis could be used for the conveyance of information that would not normally be conveyed in language poor in automorphic structures. In neurophysiological terms, the 'saved' cathexis could be used for the firing of neural messages that would not normally be fired.[10] And in psychoanalytic terms, the 'saved' cathexis could be used to overcome repression, or more precisely, to overcome the countercathexis that Freud postulated is necessary to accomplish repression.[11] Obviously, information theory, neurophysiology, and psychoanalysis all overlap here, and it is very difficult to find a vocabulary that everyone will want to hear. If we simply dispense with the jargons of various fields, we might put it this way: *devices of structural similarity in language tend to facilitate the communication of previously inaccessible information, and the reason this happens may be because the energy saved by such devices is utilized to overcome whatever it was that was making the information inaccessible in the first place.* Eventually it may be possible to measure exactly how much 'work' the automorphic structures do, and to interpolate such a measurement into equation (9). Such measurements, in turn, would enhance our understanding of the nature of repression.

NOTES

[1] The original Shannon-Weaver formula states that the entropy of a discreet set of probabilities $p_1, \ldots, p_n$ is

$$H = -\Sigma p_i \log p_i,$$

where p_i is the defining sample (Shannon & Weaver 1949:54; Revzin 1962:288).

[2] Those constraints included in β which specifically involve *repetition* of structural elements decrease information at the following rate:

$$\Delta R = - K \log_2 n,$$

which is to say: "when a perception ... is repeated n times, the rate of information yielded per unit of time decreases as the binary logarithm [logarithm to base 2] of the number of repetitions increases" (Moles 1966:154; I have simply quoted Moles' so-called "law of repetition" which he applies to the perception of musical units). Of course, as the repetitions are modified by variations (e.g., non-fulfillment of ictuses), the redundancy or information decrease caused by the repetitions is less than the equation indicates. Furthermore, as will be shown below (34), certain kinds of repetitive devices have the effect of clearing the channel and allowing for greater information transfer.

[3] Rhythmic information alone must also decrease. For example, Kondratov finds that, for a sequence where the maximum possible entropy (if there were complete randomness) would be 3.0, in a selection of iambic verse from Blok, Puškin, and Lomonosov the entropy (H_2) averages 0.91, while in a selection of Russian scientific prose the entropy is 2.38 (1969, table 2). But Bailey (1977:299) argues that Kondratov's choice of a maximum possible entropy of $H_2 = 3.0$ is not clearly motivated.

[4] The present discussion is of course also about death. How, therefore is it possible to claim that Gray's poem conveys more information about death than does the present discussion? The psychoanalytic answer is that Gray's poem, because it is laced with defensive poetic structures, brings us into direct confrontation with those semantic elements concerned with death, while the present discussion (like any discussion bereft of elaborate poetic defenses) gives us merely a "Niederschrift" ("second record" — Freud) of such semantic elements. Or, to state the matter in the terms formulated by Abraham Moles, the present discussion only conveys 'semantic information' about death, while Gray's poem conveys both 'semantic information' and 'esthetic information' about death, i.e., conveys an overall greater total of information. Moles' approach, incidentally, offers support to Lotman's claim (1971:43) that an artistic text can convey significantly more information than a non-artistic text (but Lotman does not cite Moles anywhere in his discussion).

[5] Technically speaking, information theory deals only with quantity, not with quality of information. One of the problems with the notion of β, as Bailey (1977:300) discusses, is that the relative contribution of its different components (rhyme, enjambment, rhythmical figures, etc.) is extremely difficult to determine. Moles (1966) has made some interesting attempts to convert quantitative considerations into qualitative ones. In particular he makes a valiant attempt to distinguish between 'semantic information' and 'esthetic information'. The latter is characterized by: a) untranslatability into another language or nonparaphrasability in the same language; b) lack of goal or intent; c) modification of internal mental states rather than modification of external behavior; and d) a tendency to 'overwhelm' the receiver, so that repeated reception of 'esthetic information' is required to appreciate all aspects of the message. It would seem, however, that all of these characteristics describe not a different *kind* of information, but simply 'semantic information' that has been subjected to certain mental process. Thus to say that 'esthetic information' is nonparaphrasable is no different from saying that certain semantic elements must forever remain unconscious. Furthermore, the unconsciousness of a semantic element (e.g., "I wish to slay my father") generally implies an unconsciousness of the *goal* associated with that element (". . . in order to sleep with my mother"). If Freud demonstrated anything in *The Interpretation of Dreams*, it was that the wish-fulfillment (goal-directedness, teleology) of a dream is unconscious, at least at the time of the dream. Any notion of purposelessness in signifying systems (e.g., Oscar Wilde's aestheticist view that "All art is quite useless") is but the result of repression, and flies in the face of the principle of psychical determinism which is the cornerstone of psychoanalysis. As for the notion that 'aesthetic information' modifies states of mind rather than external behavior, the psychoanalyst would say that such a modification corresponds to the activation of a

wish which cannot be acted out in reality (see Introduction to this book). Finally, the notion that 'esthetic information' 'overwhelms' the receiver seems quite true, but does not take cognizance of the *compulsion to repeat* ("Wiederholungszwang") which probably also plays a role in the receiver's tendency to repeat his reception of the message (i.e., to repeat acts of signification). Note that Moles is quite conscious of the fact that he has not been able to find a place for psychoanalysis in his information theory of esthetic perception (1966 [1958]:94, 194).

6   Lotman is quite aware of the impossibility of paraphrasing literary art, but he approaches the matter in a somewhat different manner. He suggests that elements that would be redundant in a non-literary context are for the most part recoded (cf. his "perekodirovka"), so that little or nothing in the literary text is redundant. Thus if anything is removed or changed in the literary text, information is lost, and the overall cohesiveness (cf. Tynjanov's "tesnota slovesnogo rjada") of the text is damaged. Lotman's belief that redundance "tends to zero" in literary art is part of his larger hypothesis that the information load of the literary text is considerably higher than that of a normal, non-literary text (*Lekcii po struktural'noj poètike*, 187). Such an assertion of course flatly contradicts equation (1) above, since the greater value of β in the literary text (as opposed to the non-literary text) works to *decrease* the information load in the literary text (relative to the non-literary text). I have tried to deal with this contradiction in equation (9), which separates β_1 from β_2 and leaves quite open the possibility of "perekodirovka". Another Soviet semiotician, V. A. Zareckij, perceives the problem in yet another way. He states that, although the superimposition of structural constraints decreases maximal entropy in the poetic text (relative to the non-poetic text), it nonetheless increases "meaningfulness" ("soderžatel'nost'" – 1965:71). More specifically, the ability of the text to transfer information is *not* defined by maximum possible entropy, but by the relationship between maximum entropy and real entropy. If, for example, the rhythmic variations are rich enough and the real entropy is high enough, then the "relative entropy" ("otnositel'naja èntropija") is higher in such a system than the "relative entropy" in a system that is rhythmically relatively unstructured (*ibid.*, 72).

7   The constraint operates for the duration of *The Burial of the Dead*.

8   Note that, although successful verbal art does not tolerate deviations from the constraints it establishes, the converse is not necessarily true, i.e., low tolerance to deviation from the constraints does not necessarily make successful verbal art. The sonnet form, for example, is a quite rigid set of constraints, but few poets have been able to get at repressed semantic material via these constraints as well as, say, Shakespeare did in his sonnets.

9   The neurophysiological basis for the notion of cathexis is cogently defended by Pribram (1962).

10   Perhaps the 'saved' cathexis takes the form of a catalyst.

11   The unquestionable *therapeutic* value of poetry (cf. Lerner 1976 and 1973) is intimately tied up with the lifting of repression (or partial lifting of repression) that occurs when a poem is produced or heard. Indeed the rapidly growing 'poetry therapy' movement is an excellent illustration of the psychoanalytic principle that bringing hitherto repressed material to consciousness can be therapeutic. It is not clear, however, just how much of this therapeutic effect is due to the automorphic structures in poetry, and how much is due to the fact that patients in 'poetry therapy' are provided with an environment conducive to the lifting of repression (much as the analyst's couch provides such an environment).

IV

Contiguity, Similarity, and the Tendentious Subject

Everywhere is here, once we have shattered
The iron-bound laws of contiguity.
Robert Graves

The semantic operations of contiguity and similarity are absolutely fundamental to the workings of the human mind. If, for example, I wish to compare two things, they instantly form a relationship of spatial and/or temporal contiguity in my consciousness, and I then apply the principle of similarity to the two contiguous things, i.e., I search for similarities and differences between them. Every comparison of two things requires that both contiguity and similarity operate, though of course not every two contiguous things need to be compared, which is to say they could remain merely contiguous.

To take a concrete example: a tree and a house may be either compared or they may be put into some other relationship. To compare them is to imply their contiguity in my mind (though not necessarily in the real world) before their similarity is even considered, but to make them contiguous in my mind is not necessarily to apply the principle of similarity to them. Thus I can think of a bucolic scene in which a spreading oak tree grows beside a large house and provides shelter to the birds living in it, *just as* the house provides shelter to people. Such a thought involves contiguity and similarity processes. On the other hand I can think of a tree house. Such a thought involves only a contiguity process – the house is *in* the tree, and no effort is being made to compare the house with the tree.

More generally speaking, whereas it is possible to relate two semantic elements by contiguity without applying the principle of similarity to them, it is impossible to apply the principle of similarity to two semantic elements without also relating these elements by contiguity.[1] Even the most explicit possible statement of similarity, as in

(1)   Fred is similar to Ned

implies a contiguity of the similar elements. This contiguity is emphasized in certain idiomatic expressions of similarity:

(2)   Fred is a chip *off* the old block (Fred's father is Ned),

(3)   Fred takes *after* Ned,

(4)   A little bit of Fred's cowardice rubbed *off* onto Ned,

(5)   Fred wishes he were *in* Ned's shoes,

   etc., etc.,

where the *prepositions* in particular state the manifest contiguity of elements asserted to be similar. Incidentally, the names 'Fred' and 'Ned' were deliberately chosen here to reinforce the asserted similarity, and such a choice reflects a general principle: any assertion of similarity between two or more semantic elements will be conveyed more easily or *persuasively* if the signifiers of the elements are also perceptibly similar. Consider the following minimal pairs:

(6)   A   B

   flower power   floral power

   I like Ike   I am fond of Ike

   Old enough to bleed,   Old enough to menstruate,
   old enough to breed.   old enough to reproduce.

Anyone will agree that, although each item in A has roughly the same meaning as its counterpart in B, the assertion in A is much more effective. This is because not just one, but two equations are being made, i.e., not just

(7)   flowers   = power   ('flowers represent power')

      speaker of   = Eisenhower   ('I identify with Eisen-
      utterance   hower')

menstruation = ability to ('menstruation represents
have children ability to have children')

but also

(8) [. . . awər] = [. . . awər]

[ay] = [ay . . .]

[b . . . iyd] = [b . . . iyd].

If the assertion of semantic similarity is reinforced by phonetic similarity, then the presence of phonetic similarity can lead one to
expect, under certain conditions, the assertion of semantic similarity.
That is, not only does one find that the persuasiveness of an assertion
of similarity increases with a superadded phonetic similarity, but one
can also observe that, conversely, the presence of a phonetic similarity can add a semantic similarity. This latter tendency was stated
by both a psychoanalyst and a linguist who were writing at an
interval of more than half a century from one another:

Whenever one psychical element is linked with another by an objectionable and
superficial association, there is also a legitimate and deeper link between them
which is subjected to the resistance of the censorship. (Freud, *SE* V:530)

. . . equivalence in sound, projected into the sequence as its constituitive principle, inevitably involves semantic equivalence . . . . (Jakobson 1960a:368)

The difference here is that, whereas Freud does not quite specify
that the "objectionable and superficial association" is usually phonological in nature, Jakobson does not quite specify that the "semantic
equivalence" is usually unconscious (and often censored).

The importance of the similarity/contiguity dichotomy for various
linguistic processes has been demonstrated by Jakobson (Jakobson
and Halle 1956:58ff; Jakobson 1971b:239-59). Before Jakobson the
associationist psychologists Hartley, (James) Mill, Spencer, and others
had dealt rather extensively with the topics of similarity and contiguity (Laferrière 1972:49). Ultimately the dichotomy can be traced
back to Aristotle (*De Memoria et Reminiscentia*). The similarity/
contiguity dichotomy is thus nothing particularly new in the history
of western thought.

What Jakobson did, however, was to revitalize the dichotomy in
his notion of "poetic function":

... selection is produced on the base of equivalence, similarity and dissimilarity, synonymity and antonymity, while ... combination, the build up of the sequence, is based on contiguity. *The poetic function projects the principle of equivalence from the axis of selection into the axis of combination.* Equivalence is promoted to the constituitive device of the sequence. (Jakobson 1960a:358)

Or, to state the definition more specifically in terms of the similarity/ contiguity dichotomy: the poetic function is the contamination of certain contiguity processes with similarity processes (cf. *ibid.* 370; see also above, 14, for a psychoanalytic extension of the notion of poetic function). As an example of Jakobson's conception of the poetic function, we may cite the speaker of English who decides to modify the noun 'bystander' with the adjective 'innocent': in doing so he superimposes upon the two *contiguous* words a *similarity* that is normally absent in a noun phrase, i.e., he modifies a dactylic noun that is rich in dental consonants with a dactylic adjective that is also rich in dentals.

What I wish to propose is that this contamination of contiguity processes by similarity processes does not uniquely characterize the poetic function. Rather, contiguity tends to be accompanied by similarity in all 'non-logical' or 'pre-logical' thinking in human beings. Magical thinking, dreams, and figurative language will here be taken as specific examples.

Let us begin with three examples of magical thinking:

(9)   In Aleksandr Solženicyn's novel *V kruge pervom* (*In the First Circle*) the Soviet secret police wish to perpetrate the myth that the wives of political prisoners, like the prisoners themselves, must be 'enemies of the people'.

(10) A little boy may sometimes experience a block against urinating, especially if one of the parents has requested that he urinate. One way to overcome the block is to turn on a water faucet in the vicinity.

(11) The transsubstantiation which took place at the last supper is described as follows: "And while they were still at table, Jesus took bread, and blessed, and broke it, and gave it to them, saying, Take this; this is my body. Then he took a cup, and offered thanks, and gave it to them, and they all drank of it. And he said, this is my blood of the new testament, shed for many." (Mark 14:22-24)

The common principle uniting these rather diverse examples of magical thinking is this: what began as a relationship of mere contiguity is eventually thought of as a relationship of similarity as well. Thus certain people who were at one time contiguous with the prisoners become similar to the prisoners (they become "guilty by association", as it were). An action contiguous to the boy, the flow of water from a long object, induces a similar action by the boy, the flow of urine from his penis.[2] Christ asserts that the food and drink contiguous to him becomes similar enough to him to represent him. In each case some semantic element X (wives of prisoners, boy's penis, bread and wine) is assimilated to some semantic element Y (prisoners, water faucet, Christ's body and blood).

Assimilations of this type basically follow the pattern established in what Sir James George Frazer terms "homoeopathic or imitative magic", i.e., magic based on what he calls the "Law of Similarity" (Frazer 1951 [1922] : 14ff.). One of Frazer's examples is the following:

... when an Ojebway Indian desires to work evil on any one, he makes a little wooden image of his enemy and runs a needle into its head or heart, or he shoots an arrow into it, believing that wherever the needle pierces or the arrow strikes the image, his foe will the same instant be seized with a sharp pain in the corresponding part of his body; but if he intends to kill the person outright, he burns or buries the puppet, uttering certain magic words as he does so. (*ibid.* 15)

Even in what Frazer terms "contagious magic", i.e., magic based on the "Law of Contact or Contagion", similarity is superimposed upon what was originally a semantic contiguity:

In Sussex some fifty years ago a maid-servant remonstrated strongly against the throwing away of children's cast teeth, affirming that should they be found and gnawed by any animal, the child's new tooth would be, for all the world, like the teeth of the animal that had bitten the old one. In proof of this she named old Master Simmons, who had a very large pig's tooth in his upper jaw, a personal defect that he always averred was caused by his mother, who threw away one of his cast teeth by accident into the hog's trough. (*ibid.* 44)

Whereas in homoeopathic magic the object of the magical act never came into actual contact with what it signifies, in contagious magic the object began by being in physical contact with what it signifies (e.g., the magical object is a tooth, hair, fingernails, umbilical cord, etc. of the person represented). But in both kinds of magic a semantic contiguity leads to a semantic similarity, an assimilation is made. The wooden image of the enemy is semantically contiguous to the enemy, though it may never have been contiguous to the enemy in the real world, whereas the cast tooth happens to have been both physically as well as semantically contiguous with the child (and the animal).

We may schematicize these various assimilations as follows:

(12)

X	assimilates to	Y
a) wives of prisoners		prisoners
b) boy's penis		water faucet
c) bread and wine		Christ's body and blood
d) enemy		wooden image of enemy
e) new tooth		tooth of animal

The fact that subjects assimilate X to Y rather than to some other element, say, Z, is not accidental. For one thing, Z may be so semantically remote that any attempt at imposing a similarity would be thought of as absurd or irrelevant. For example, if the little boy in question were to turn the bathroom mirror upside down rather than turn on the water faucet, he would probably not be able to urinate.[3] There have to be some minimal tertia comparationes (which I will hereafter call shared properties) for the imposed similarity to be effective for the subject who imposes the similarity. Thus, for the boy to urinate, the shared properties have to be something like: a roughly cylindrical shape, from which a liquid can flow. On the other hand, the presence of shared properties does not at all guarantee that an assimilation will be made, for 1) a comparable semantic element may not be or may never have been in the subject's consciousness (e.g., if the boy has never heard of the "Fountain of Arethusa" in Greek mythology, then the objective similarity between this fountain and the boy's penis will not help the boy urinate), and 2) a comparable element may be present but still not have anything to do with the underlying motivation or psychological center of action (e.g., both the boy's penis and the boy's left elbow are covered with skin, but this shared property does not relate to the boy's problem). The need for considering motivation or a psychological center of action in the genesis of similarity processes was clearly recognized by the Hungarian psychoanalyst Sandor Ferenczi in 1913:

... one was formerly inclined to believe that things are confounded because they are similar; nowadays we know that a thing is confounded with another only because certain motives for this are present; *similarity merely provides the opportunity for these motives to function.* (Ferenczi 1952 [1913] :281, emphasis added)

Now, the study of motivation (desire, need, disgust, etc.) may at first glance appear to fall outside the province of the semiotician who is studying similarity and contiguity processes. In fact, however, it is impossible to ignore motivation when answering even the simplest and most basic questions about similarity-contiguity interaction. For example, we observed that X assimilates to Y, but what is there to prevent the subject from performing the opposite operation, "Y assimilates to X?" More concretely, what is it that makes the following assimilations incorrect?

(13   a) The prisoners assimilate to the wives of the prisoners
       b) The water faucet assimilates to the boy's penis.
       c) Christ's body and blood assimilates to the bread and wine.
       d) The wooden image of the enemy assimilates to the enemy.
       e) The animal's tooth assimilates to the person's new tooth.

The answer is that in each case the assimilation is exactly the opposite to the direction of the subject's wish (or is only an intermediate step in the accomplishment of the wish). Technically speaking, of course, each of the assimilations in (13) is 'correct', for if X is similar to Y, then Y has to be similar to X as well: every assimilation rests on a logical double entailment. But *the wish concentrates on only one half of the entailment*. Thus Solženicyn's secret police are not particularly interested in assimilating the prisoners to the wives of the prisoners, for that would not accomplish the wish, namely, the wish to sadistically harass more Soviet citizens. Similarly, the Ojebway who carves a wooden effigy of his enemy is not particularly interested in perfecting the similarity of the piece of wood to the enemy (Y assimilates to X), but focuses his attention on the wish that the enemy be the piece of wood (X assimilates to Y to the point of identity). Such omission of logical entailments is of course quite common in wishful thinking of all kinds, as in the Russian proverb "Net xuda bez dobra" ("There is no evil without good"), which suppresses the logically entailed "Net dobra bez xuda" ("There is no good without evil"). The same is true of the more 'quasi-' or 'para-' logical entailments, e.g., "When the sun goes down, so do our prices" (*TWA* advertisement) suppresses "When the sun comes up, so do our prices"; "It's always darkest before the dawn" suppresses something like "It's always brightest before the night".

The conclusion I reached in my analysis of the basic dream processes (Laferrière 1972) is that each of these processes involves the super-imposition of semantic similarity upon semantic contiguity. Thus SYMBOLISM (Freudian, not Peircian) consists of a failure to per-ceive the 'activated' similarity between two semantically contiguous elements, such as a snake and a penis, a cave and a vagina, an ice cream cone and a breast, etc. (again the similarity is one-directional, e.g., what is important is that a snake is similar to a penis, not *vice-versa*, otherwise we would have penises symbolizing snakes, which would be 'badly defended' symbolism). The failure of the dreaming subject to perceive the similarity is tantamount to his *repression* of the symbolized element, but does not annihilate the semiosis which results from the similarity. The subject's attention and affect are merely *displaced* (for defensive reasons) along an axis of contiguity away from the unconscious symbolized element toward the conscious symbol. In Peircian terms the symbol is an 'unintentional iconic sign' − iconicity being a species of semantic similarity (Jakobson 1970b:10; cf. Charles Morris 1946:276, who speaks of dream sym-bols as "general icons"; also Jean Piaget 1962:169, who observes that symbols have a "direct resemblence between signifier and signified"). Ernest Jones, in his fundamental paper on dream symbolism (1913), has established the relatively narrow repertoire of things that can be symbolized − basically the body parts, members of the dreamer's immediate family, birth, love, and death.

In CONDENSATION the repertoire is much less limited. In Freud's dream of the injection of Irma, for example, Irma un-consciously represented quite a few people, i.e., she was a condensation or collection of properties shared with (or 'activated similarities' to) many people in Freud's life.

In IDENTIFICATION the semantic similarity is projected specifi-cally between two persons. For example, the dreamer may not find himself anywhere in the manifest content of the dream, but close examination usually shows that he is identified with some other character. The dreamer has, in other words, unconsciously projected or 'activated' a similarity between himself and a contiguous character.

All three major processes of the dream-work − symbolism, con-densation, and identification − involve the projection of a similarity between one conscious semantic element and one or more other contiguous unconscious semantic elements. Viewed semiotically, this projection constitutes an icon. All three major dream processes are icons (Bateson 1968 has also examined dream icons). To claim that the basic dream processes are icons, however, is to raise the whole knotty issue of the validity of the notion of 'icon' – an issue that cannot be treated in depth here. It seems that, although some have retained and elaborated this Peircian notion, others have rejected it totally (for an overview of the problem, see Sebeok 1976). A particularly notable modification of the notion of icon is Eco's claim, which must necessarily follow from his rejection of an extensional semantics, that iconicity is primarily the result of cultural norms, not objective similarities or shared properties (Eco 1976:191ff.). For purposes of the present discussion, I shall try to avoid the thorny issues by making the following assumptions: the operation of an icon will never be explained only by enumerating the number and kinds of qualities which must be shared between signifier and signified; on the other hand it will never be sufficient to observe that signifier and signified are united only by cultural convention. What is required is a recognition of the fact that the universe is populated with similarities, physically and culturally determined, and that these similarities merely wait for signifying subjects to come along and transform them into icons. The difference between a mere similarity and an icon is the addition of a tendentious interpreter. Psychoanalytically, this transformation of similarity into iconicity amounts to a utilization of semantic similarities for the purpose of fulfilling a wish (Freud's original theory of the dream as *wish-fulfillment* is crucial to distinguishing similarity from iconicity in the oneiric context).

What is interesting about the projection of similarity to form dream icons is that one or more elements involved in the similarity is always repressed, at least until the dream is analyzed (whereupon the repressed element is made conscious, though not necessarily unrepressed, i.e., a mere "Niederschrift" of the repressed semantic element is likely to be established in the waking, analytic consciousness). The reason for the repression, psychoanalysis teaches, is that extreme unpleasure would result if the repression were to be lifted completely. The direct, unmitigated expression of a repressed semantic element would be highly 'ego-distonic', and it is considered more 'ego-syntonic' for the repressed element to be only indirectly expressed via another contiguous element which shares semantic properties with the repressed element. For example, in the dream of Irma's injection Irma possesses a diphtheretic spot, and this is because Freud's daughter Mathilde was once gravely ill with diphtheria: rather than deal directly with the ego-distonic semantic elements surrounding the illness and potential death of his daughter, Freud instead dreams of finding diphtheria in *another* person who is not nearly so important to him as his daughter. By establishing a certain distance (*semantic contiguity*) between the dangerous semantic elements (thoughts of his daughter's death) and the relatively harmless semantic elements (thoughts of diphtheria in his patient Irma), Freud manages to escape from or defend himself against the dangerous semantic elements. On the other hand, by maintaining a *semantic similarity* (expressible as the shared property of diphtheria) between the dangerous semantic elements and the relatively harmless ones, Freud nonethless manages to signify the dangerous semantic elements. Thus the contiguity between the two kinds of semantic elements establishes the defensive measure, while the similarity between the elements establishes a semiosis (iconic). *The contiguity is to the similarity as the defense is to the semiosis.*

The three major processes of the dream-work may now be represented as follows:

(14)

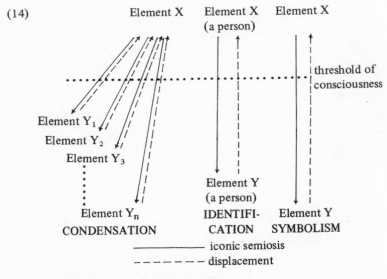

The downward arrows represent the direction of *iconic semiosis*, i.e., from some semantic element X in consciousness during the dream toward some semantic element(s) Y not in consciousness during the dream (except in some nightmares, where element Y may come very close to being conscious). The upward arrows represent the direction of the *displacement* of the dreamer's attention and affect. In the 'topography' ("Topik") of the mental apparatus the semiosis is thus in some sense opposed to the displacement. If this opposition did not exist, i.e., if the arrows went only in one direction, then we would have either 1) pure, unhampered semiosis (arrows only downward) in which the signified element(s) Y is conscious, as in the usual explicit use of icons (e.g., the English verb "deflower," in which the iconic relationship of plant genitalia to human genitalia is actually explicit), or 2) we would have pure repression (arrows only upward) in which the displacement of attention and affect away from Y is so thorough that not even the semiotic connection between X and Y remains. The only example of pure repression is complete unconsciousness, all other forms of repression being contaminated by semiosis (e.g., the convulsive hysteric is not adequately managing to repress element Y because she also iconically signifies it with her *arc de cercle*).   ·

Theoretically, semiotics studies the mechanisms by means of which the arrows such as those in (14) point downward from signifier X to signified Y, whereas psychoanalysis studies both the mechanisms by means of which the arrows point downward (from signifier X to signified Y) as well as the mechanisms by means of which the arrows point upward (from repressed element Y to conscious element X). In practice, however, semioticians have tended to avoid oneiric and other signs involving a repressed signified (unless we arbitrarily define as semioticians the scholars who, like Freud, Pötzl, Silberer, Piaget, and others, have studied such signs: see Richard Jones 1970 for an overview of dream studies since Freud). Conversely, psychoanalysts have tended not to see dream processes from a specifically semiotic viewpoint. A notable exception to this latter tendency, however, is Jacques Lacan, who borrows from the Saussurian model of a sign:

(15) $\dfrac{S}{s}$,

where S is a signifier (*signifiant*) and s a signified (*signifié*) in any discourse (including dream narration), and the line separating the two is the repression that makes the semiosis unconscious ("−", "la barre", "la barrière résistante à la signification" − 1966:497). Because every S has its own meaning s within conscious discourse (e.g., the word "snake" refers to a snake as well as being able to refer to a penis), then Lacan expands his diagram as follows:

(16) $\dfrac{\dfrac{S}{s}}{\dfrac{S}{s}}$.

I avoid this kind of schematization because 1) it in no way represents the opposition between semiosis and displacement, and 2) it implies that the signified s requires a discursive signifier S when in fact there may be no discourse at all, i.e., the subject may never utter his dream and the signification make take place exclusively between s's (e.g., the notion of a snake [semantic element X] may signify the notion of a penis [semantic element Y] without an acoustic signifier S ever being heard: indeed, if we were to claim that the snake does not signify a penis unless the dream is narrated, then we would be caught in the old philosophical trap of having to claim that the tree does not fall in the forest unless it is heard). For further discussion and critique of Lacan's work, see Bär 1974; Meschonnic 1975:314-22; Laferrière 1977b. Generally speaking, Lacan's quasi-Saussurian scheme for relating signifier and signified is one instance where the catch-as-catch-can approach advocated above (12) fails to yield any results.

Let us now summarize the various kinds of iconic signification that have been discussed (TC = threshold of consciousness):

(17)

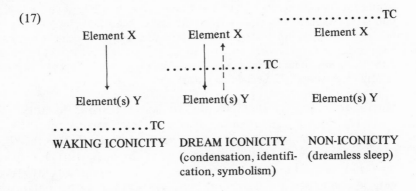

WAKING ICONICITY   DREAM ICONICITY   NON-ICONICITY
                    (condensation, identifi- (dreamless sleep)
                    cation, symbolism)

Note that when the threshold of consciousness directly intervenes between element X and element(s) Y the subject is in the peculiar state of "having his cake and eating it too": on the one hand he manages to signify Y and thereby usually accomplish a wish, while on the other hand he is defended from the ego-distonic consequences of Y. For example, if the dreaming subject wishes that a certain person Q should die, he may dream that Q departs on a train. In so dreaming the subject both fantasizes the fulfillment of his wish and disassociates himself from his wish via a semantic element X 'departure of person Q on a train' which shares the property 'departure' or 'going away' with the dangerous element Y, 'departure of person Q from this world'. By means of the similarity process the dreamer is in effect asserting that X is Y (so that the assertion of X is the assertion of Y); by means of the contiguity process, however, he is asserting that X is *not* Y (so that the assertion of X is not the assertion of Y). *In dream icons similarity is to contiguity as affirmation is to negation.*

Metaphor in the literary work of art also uses contiguity processes to accomplish a negation. Such a notion of metaphor was expressed by Robert Musil in *Der Mann Ohne Eigenschaften*, which incidentally is not only an excellent novel, but a lush garden of literary theory as well:

> ... when he [the "practical realist" Count Leinsdorf] wants to rise above the rut of every day he will resort to metaphor and simile. Obviously because snow is at times disagreeable to him, he compares it to women's glittering breasts, and as soon as his wife's breasts begin to bore him, he compares them to glimmering snow; he would be horrified if one day he and his 'little turtle dove' suddenly had horny bills to coo with, or if her lips really turned into coral, but poetically he finds it stimulating. He is capable of turning everything into anything — snow into skin, skin into blossoms, blossoms into sugar, sugar into powder, and powder back into little drifts of snow — for all that matters to him, apparently, is *to make things into what they are not*, which is doubtless proof that he cannot stand being anywhere for long, wherever he happens to be. (English translation by Wilkins & Kaiser 1953; emphasis added)

Metaphor seeks out the semantic *similarity* ("semic identity", in Eco's terminology) in semantically *contiguous* elements, but the very contiguity of the elements is paradoxically always *negating* the similarity (specifically, identity), so that what the poet affirms is always false and makes him into a 'liar'. One cannot turn breasts into snow without commiting a falsehood, without attempting to violate the Aristotelian principle of (non-)contradiction. On the other hand, as Sir Philip Sidney declared, ". . . the Poet, he nothing affirmeth, and therefore he never lieth", which in the present context means that the poet's superimposition of similarity upon contiguity is not intended to refer to the real world. In Loewenberg's terminology, since the metaphorical utterance "fails as an assertion" (= is technically false), it should be understood instead as a special kind of speech act for which falsifiability is irrelevant, i.e., as a "proposal" (Loewenberg 1975:336). Specifically, an indicative sentence is metaphorical when it fulfills two conditions: 1) it is an assertion if and only if it is false; 2) it is not an assertion (*ibid.* 337). This paradoxical state of affairs, incidentally, provides an interesting test of Eco's definition of semiotics: "... semiotics is in principle the discipline studying everything which can be used in order to lie" (1976:7): "every time there is a possibility of lying, there is a sign function ..." (*ibid.* 58). Since a metaphor must, by Loewenberg's condition 1), be used to tell a lie, then it does fit Eco's notion of a sign function and does fall within the domain of semiotics. Indeed, the study of metaphor and other tropes is that branch of semiotics which is *obliged* to deal with lies. On the other hand, since a metaphor cannot by Loewenberg's condition 2) be used to tell a lie, then metaphor does not fall within the domain of semiotics. This latter paradox itself 'mimics' the paradox with which we began, i.e., the paradox that a metaphor both asserts and negates a semantic similarity process (identity).

We can escape these paradoxes only if we ask teleological questions: *why* are the poet's 'false assertions' made?: what *do* the poet's metaphorical 'proposals' refer to, if not some objective reality? Such questions are not answered in a linguistic (e.g., a transformationalist or Katzian semantic) approach to metaphor, nor does Loewenberg pretend to answer such questions with her philosophical formula. The questions can be fruitfully discussed, however, within a psychoanalytic context.

Basically, the psychoanalyst would claim that metaphors make assertions about repressed material in the unconscious (which material we may again represent as semantic element(s) Y). The very fact that the poet wants us to take his 'falsehood' as in some sense 'true' already indicates that what he is saying is somehow out of the reach of his conscious signifying ability. The poet cannot really say what he means, he cannot unrepress some element Y and is therefore obliged to assert some false *but similar* element instead. But what is the nature of this similarity?

Let us imagine that a lyric poet is in a situation where old fantasies about his mother's breast are reactivated (he is 'inspired' by something that unconsciously reminds him of an archaic attachment to the breast). First he may distance himself from such fantasies by inventing another speaker, another 'I', such as a lyric persona or a character other than the lyric persona. Then, still unable to express the particular semantic element Y ('mother's breast') because of its ego-distonic implications, he will perhaps speak of snow instead (semantic element X, related by iconic semiosis to semantic element Y). This being unsatisfactory, however, he will bring in still other elements (X_2, X_3, etc.) similar to the first — his wife's breasts, blossoms, sugar, powder, etc., but never will a semantic element X be exactly identical to element Y, never will the poet actually assert Y, which is to say that no metaphor is ever 'adequate', and that the poet is therefore condemned to perpetually move from metaphor to metaphor, "to make things into what they are *not*", as Musil says. This forced movement is the semiotic basis for such Romantic commonplaces as "words cannot express how I feel", "you'll never know how much I love you", etc., etc. In this movement, however, the properties of the various X's accumulate in such a way as to give the semiotician a pretty good idea of what the underlying Y is. In the example at hand the elements X_2 ('wife's breast') and X_4 ('sugar') are particularly revealing because their juxtaposition generates the notion of actually receiving nourishment from a breast, i.e., a notion that was for the subject literally true of the mother's breast and no one else's breast. The assemblage of X's, all ultimately pointing to a 'deeper' Y, may be diagrammed as follows (for legend, see (14)):

(18)

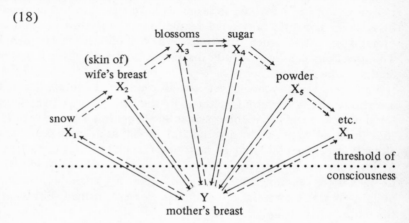

The series of displacements and semioses from X_1 to X_n is based, as Count Leinsdorf perfectly well knows, on *boredom*. What our aristocratic lyricist does not know, however, and what most lyric poets would rather not know, is that the movement from X_1 to X_n is accompanied by a series of paired displacements and semioses based on *danger*. The superficial similarities (tertia comparationes normally studied in handbooks of rhetoric) mask a more profound complex of similarities that relate to a dangerous or ego-distonic element Y. Psychoanalysts are accustomed to looking for just such an element when the patient is suffering from extreme boredom: to be bored with external reality very often signals a threat from the internal world.

The displacements from metaphor to metaphor can take the form of negation. Thus, to paraphrase Count Leinsdorf: "My wife's breast is (like) glimmering snow; no, it is (like) blossoms; no, it is (like) sugar; no, it is (like) powder; no, it is... etc., etc." Ultimately, Count Leinsdorf is at a loss for words: "To what shall I compare thee?", he in effect asks, and can never find an adequate answer, as in the Romantic commonplace "Nothing can compare...". But this 'nothing', this series of negations which becomes more and more suspect as it grows (cf. Shakespeare's "The lady doth protest too much") is just an imitation of the implicit negation which set the whole chain of metaphors into motion, namely: "No, my wife's breast is not like my mother's breast. Rather, it is like snow, powder, etc., etc." If it were possible for the poet to say what he really means ("Kak beden naš jazyk!" – Afanasij Fet) rather than negate what he means via the accumulating contiguities, i.e., if the outright expression of semantic element Y were not ego-distonic, then he would have no need for metaphor (or more generally, for figurative language). As it is, he cannot say what he means, therefore he 'suggests' it instead with an accumulation of tropes that never suffices, he furnishes a chain of fore-pleasures without any end-pleasure except perhaps the pseudo-end-pleasure of the poem's symmetrical closure.

There is a curious parallel between the chain of implicit negations which build up in metaphorical discourse and a chain of negations that grows in argumentative discourse:

... in order to support my thesis statement I must make another statement, and in order to support this statement, I must make still others. The mere act of extending outwards into discursive space statements followed by still other statements needed to support these, fragments my central statement into a sequential manifold of syntactic strings. In further specifying the line of argument advanced by previous statements, each succeeding statement modifies them in some way, and denies their implicit claim to being at that point the "final" one that need be made. And so, what we usually think of as "wellformed discourse," a harmonious flow of logical entailments, discloses itself as actually *a series of denials*, of announcements that *"No, that's not quite it* – we must say something further." (McCanles 1975:4, emphasis added)

McCanles adds:

The urge to create a "universal philosophy" is ... the urge to "use up" all discursive space, so that no other statements save those coherently flowing from the original *données* of their systems could find a place in it. As the anagogical extension of oral fixation, it is the urge, finally, to swallow up the whole of reality in a single, vast tautology. (*ibid.* 7)

Both metaphorical and argumentative types of discourse thrive on successions of negations (recall also that the very definition of a sign is also based on a negation — above, 12-14). But whereas metaphorical discourse spawns its negations because of the poet's original inability to make an ego-distonic statement, argumentative discourse advances by negation because of the philosopher's original inability to make a perfectly 'analytic statement' (according to Kant, an 'analytic statement' is [roughly] one whose meaning and truth is immediately and intuitively evident, and which therefore does not require further discourse). An ego-distonic statement is in metaphorical discourse what an analytic statement is in philosophical discourse, i.e., a rarity. Whereas all metaphorical (figurative) discourse aspires to an ego-distonic proposition, *and fails*, "all [argumentative] discourse aspires to the analytic proposition, *and fails*" (*ibid.* 1, emphasis added). Moreover, both metaphorical and argumentative discourse constitute an "anagogical extension of oral fixation" (cf. Brill 1931). The difference is that, whereas the urge to make metaphors is based on the urge to imitate reality (similarity processes superimposed upon contiguity processes), "the urge to create a 'universal philosophy'" is based on the urge to "swallow up the whole of reality" (contiguity processes only). Psychoanalysts will of course detect the parallel between this latter distinction and the frequent distinction that is made between identification vs. introjection (incorporation). Or, to speak in terms of yet another psychoanalytic distinction, we may say that the poet forms a narcissistic attachment to his (internal or external) object ("I want to be *like* you"), while the philosopher forms an anaclitic attachment to his object ("I want to *have* you").

A concrete example will help clarify further differences between metaphorical and argumentative discourse:

(19)   Every man is mortal.
        Socrates is a man.
        _____
        ∴ Socrates is mortal.

Such is the manner in which a syllogism operates in argumentative discourse. In metaphorical discourse, however, we are just as likely to find:

(20)   Every man is mortal.
        Socrates is a man.
        _____
        ∴ Every man is Socrates.

or

(21)   Every man is mortal.
         Socrates is a man.
         ─────────────────────
         ∴ I am Socrates.

That is, the poet does not feel so restrained as the philosopher in imposing similarity processes upon contiguity processes. Whereas the
philosopher can only allow one proposition to flow from his two
premises, i.e., his logic can permit only the one shared property
(similarity process) of 'mortality' between the (semantically contiguous) 'Socrates' and 'every man', the poet will permit all sorts of
additional similarities as well. For example, if the poet wishes to
assert that every man must face death, he may conclude that every
man is Socrates – an assertion that is objectively false, but which
asks us to *identify* with Socrates, i.e., to project an additional similarity process. The poet is saying that, not only with respect to
'mortality', but in all respects we are to think of ourselves as Socrates.
Only then can we begin to comprehend the enormity of death
because only then can we conceive of Socrates' death as our own.
From the mere "Niederschrift" of death in the innocuous word
'mortality' we move closer to real contemplation of death. If the
poet then says "I am Socrates", we move even closer, for the first
person pronoun clinches the identification and reminds us (another
similarity process) that we too use first person pronouns. But the
poet does not say "I will die", i.e., he does not state the ego-distonic
proposition directly because few of us can bear it without a wealth
of similarity processes attached to it. Only the hardiest of egos can
contemplate what really happened to Socrates. Others have to be
satisfied with philosophy ('every man is *mortal*') or with poetry
('every man is *Socrates*').

The relevance of the similarity/contiguity dichotomy to figurative
language has of course already been observed by Jakobson, who
states:

The development of a discourse may take place along two different semantic
lines: one topic may lead to another either through their similarity or through
their contiguity. The *metaphoric way* would be the most appropriate term for
the first case and the *metonymic way* for the second, since they find their most
condensed expression in metaphor and metonymy respectively. (Jakobson and
Halle 1956:76)

We should keep in mind that the distinction between "metaphoric way" and "metonymic way" was not intended by Jakobson to be very precise. Indeed the distinction between metaphor and metonymy has never been precisely delineated, nor have the various other terms that appear in the handbooks (synecdoche, catachresis, hypallage, anastrophe, etc., etc.) ever recieved a successful systematic analysis. The immense wealth of information stored in Lausberg's *Handbuch der literarischen Rhetorik* has yet to be dealt with by an adequate theory of semantics, as Professor Jakobson mentioned in one of his lectures. The terminology that is available is simply not adequate. Metaphor and metonymy are said to overlap to the extent that ". . . any metonymy is slightly metaphorical and any metaphor has a metonymical tint" (Jakobson 1960:370); compare ". . . a metonymy, even at its original creation in literary texts, is already on the way to becoming a metaphor" (Shapiro 1976:12). And in the psychoanalytic context we find that the very same events in a dream can be interpreted as both metaphoric and metonymic (Bär 1974; 504-08; further psychoanalytic study of metaphor/metonymy is given by Rosolato 1974). In particular the notion of metaphor is too vague and covers a multitude of sins, most of them confessed by Ricoeur in his immense treatise *La métaphore vive* (1975). Above I have also deliberately used the term 'metaphor' or 'metaphorical language' in the vague sense of any figurative language.

What *is* precise, however, is the similarity/contiguity opposition. Although the opposition defies definition, it is intuitively evident (just as mass, distance, and time are undefinable but intuitively evident to the physicist who deals with them in very precise ways). The opposition should thus be more useful for doing further research on figurative language than the metaphor/metonymy dichotomy. It is more basic and underlies *both* metaphor and metonymy. More specifically, both metaphor and metonymy superimpose similarity upon contiguity. In what most people would accept as a 'metaphor', this is easy to see: the expression "head of the penis" superimposes a similarity (shared semantic property) between the semantically contiguous items, penis and body as a whole. In what would possibly be accepted as the most important 'metonymy' of the unconscious, this superimposition is perhaps more difficult to see: psychoanalysts (e.g., Ferenczi 1972 II:351) speak of the *pars pro toto* function of the phallus, which is another way of saying that there is a tendency for subjects to project a similarity (viz., identity) between the penis and the whole person with whom it is contiguous (some languages, such as Armenian, even allow the dimunitive of a man's name to refer to the man's penis; fetishism and Kleinian 'partial objects' could also be studied from the viewpoint of the similarity/contiguity opposition).

Let us note that the similarity/contiguity opposition is illustrated not only by the figurative level of literary discourse, but by other levels as well. For example, the narrative devices of pathetic fallacy and nature parallelism make the natural setting reflect (= be similar to) the actions and moods of the characters in (= contiguous with) that setting. In Karamzin's *Bednaja Liza* a wild thunderstorm accompanies the lovemaking of Liza and Erast, i.e., 'nature in storm' reinforces the 'stormy passions' of the hero and heroine. Not only the natural setting, but also the man-made environment may be made parallel to the characters. A particularly striking example is Gogol's character Sobakevič in *Mertvye Duši*:

All the pieces of furniture were strong, clumsy in the highest degree, and bore a strange resemblance to the master of the house; in the corner of the room stood a paunchy walnut bureau on four ridiculous legs, a perfect bear of a bureau [Sobakevič is described as a bear]. The table, the armchairs, the chairs — all were of heavy and uncomfortable make; in a word, each object, each chair seemed to be saying: "I am a Sobakevich too!" or "I too resemble Sobakevich a lot!" (Ch. VI of Michailoff translation)

One could hardly ask for a more graphic demonstration of the principle that contiguity tends to breed similarity.

To briefly summarize: when the subject engages in such practices as magical thinking, dreaming, and literary creation he tends to superimpose similarity processes upon what otherwise might be left well enough alone as contiguity processes. These similarity processes might not in fact be superimposed by the subject so much as they are observed by the subject, i.e., the subject may claim that the similarities as simply 'there'. Baudelaire made such a claim for the spatial realm when he spoke of the world as a collection of "forêts de symboles". Goethe made such a claim for the temporal realm when he declared "Alles vergängliche ist nur ein Gleichnis" (alliteratively translated by Jakobson as "anything sequent is a simile" — 1960a: 370). But whether the similarities are projected or merely observed by the subject makes no difference from the psychoanalytic viewpoint: the fact that the similarities are 'activated' already indicates the tendentiousness of the subject. That is, similarity processes in magical thinking, dreaming, and literary creation always act in the service of a wishful ego.

NOTES

[1] This state of affairs led some of the associationist psychologists to claim that association by similarity is only a special case of association by contiguity. Peirce knew better, however, and in his discussion of the topic of association he retains the similarity/contiguity opposition (*Collected Papers* VII:249-283).

[2] Compare the report of a friend who says that, whenever she needs a good cry, she draws a bath.

[3] I inadvertently made this comparison less absurd by stating it in the form of a syllepsis — or perhaps not inadvertently, but in accordance with the principle that contiguity breeds similarity.

V

The Subject and Discrepant Use of the Category of Person

> I think I'm spooked. I'm full of voices,
> all mine, none me; I can't keep straight
> who's speaking, as I used to.
>
> John Barth, *Chimera*

Any investigation into the subject's relationship with his message has to sooner or later deal with *shifters*, i.e., with those units which ". . . are distinguished from all other constituents of the linguistic code solely by their compulsory reference to the given message" (Jakobson 1971b:132; cf. Jespersen 1949:123-24). The shifters, roughly equivalent to Russell's "egocentric particulars", Quine's and Goodman's "indicator words", Heidegger's "Dasein-designations", Peirce's "indexical symbols", and Benveniste's "termes afférents à l'énonciation" (Jakobson, 1971b:2; Wilden 1968:183-85; Russell 1940:108-15; Quine 1960:101; Heidegger 1962:155-56; Buchler 1940:101-15; Benveniste 1974:79-88) include such linguistic categories as person, mood, tense, etc. Of these, the category of *person* (Filmore's "person deixis") tends to be more directly associated with the speaking subject than the other shifters. For example, the pronoun 'I' in English points explicitly to the subject, while a past tense morpheme or a conditional auxiliary points to the subject only by implication.

The category of person, moreover, presupposes certain adverbial shifters that point toward or away from the subject. Thus a sentence like

(1) *I am there then

is deviant (assuming 'point of view' doesn't change) because the shifters 'there' and 'then' predicated of the shifter 'I' contradict the 'hereness' and 'nowness' *already* denoted by an unpredicated 'I'. (Compare James Harris' assertion of an "implied presence" in the pronouns 'I' and 'you'; Harris 1751:77; Joly 1972:12). The only way to escape the contradiction in (1) is to add another shifter, e.g., marked (non-present) tense:

(2) I was / will be there then.

The tense shifter adds new information to the 'hereness' and 'nowness' already signified by the person shifter 'I'. That is, it modifies the originally direct and instantaneous relationship between the speaking subject and the person shifter which signifies that subject.[1] Indeed the marked tense shifter transforms that subject from a momentary entity into a temporal continuum. What I have been calling the 'subject' expands to what some philosophers and rhetoricians call the 'self'. To make an analogy: the person shifter is to a Euclidean point as the marked tense shifter is to a Euclidean locus of points. But this continuous locus sometimes manages to connect very different entities, as in

(7) I_1 swear I_2 could ride a horse when I_2 was four years old.

When hearing such an utterance the addressee assumes that there is some real connection between the adult addresser in the speech event and the child in the narrated event, however different the adult and the child might appear if it were possible to juxtapose them simultaneously. The use of marked tense ('could', 'was') prevents us from *literally* identifying the referent of the subject of the verb of the narrated event (Newman's "RESUVENE" − 1974) with the addresser in the speech event. Or to view the matter in a slightly different light, the use of marked tense makes us realize that 'I_1', the subject of a performative verb, cannot be *perfectly* coreferential with 'I_2', the subject of two verbs of the narrated event. More generally speaking, the use of marked tense subverts the fictitious atemporality perpetrated by the category of person. Just as the changing and unpredictable behavior of any human being can militate against the epithets affixed to him ("your miser of a father", "she whose fury pursued you through childhood"), so too the category of marked tense can militate against the fixity of the person pronouns (for an interesting discussion of the notion of 'person' in rhetoric, see

Perelman & Olbrechts-Tyteca 1969:293-305; cf. also Shands 1971: 86).
For Russian verbs, Jakobson divides the category of person into a) personal vs. impersonal, and b), within personal, first person vs. second person (1971b:137). Compare Benveniste's general classification of pronouns: "la 'troisième personne' représente en fait le membre non marqué de la corrélation de personne" (1966:255); the marked member is in turn divided by a "polarité des personnes" which opposes the speaking *I* against the *Thou* (*ibid.*, 260; Barthes 1970:139; cf. Huxley 1970, Joly 1973, and Waryas 1973 for somewhat different classifications). A working scheme for the category of (singular) person in the verbs and personal pronouns of many languages may thus be diagrammed as follows:

(8)

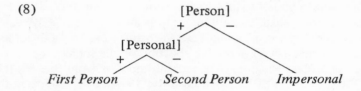

Items classified as [+person] in this scheme commonly refer to participants in the speech event (exophoric reference), while items classified as [−person] commonly refer to someone or something mentioned in the discourse proper (endophoric reference, including anaphora: see Brecht 1974:513-14).
Against this relatively cut-and-dried linguistic system for the category of person we must juxtapose the rather elusive psychoanalytic notion of the subject:

Where is the subject? It is necessary to find the subject as a lost object. More precisely this lost object is the support of the subject and in many cases is a more abject thing than you may care to consider — in some cases it is something done, as all psychoanalysts and many people who have been psychoanalyzed know perfectly well. (Lacan 1970:189)

Behind this apparent double talk is the assumption that there are at least two subjects. The 'true' or 'absolute' subject is unconscious, is lost in childhood, and in adulthood is continually 'fading' as Lacan says, under a chain of obscuring signifiers. By its tendency to repeat or split itself ("Ichspaltung" − Freud) it generates the second and any subsequent subjects (*ibid.*, 191-94; Lacan 1966:285, 372, 656, 689, 732; Wilden 1968:177-83). Comprising what is customarily termed the 'ego' (the "me" in Schneiderman's improved translation of "das Ich" — 1974:80), the second subject(s) may be so well integrated and so well isolated from the first subject as to sustain the illusion that there never was a break with the first subject, or indeed that there never was a first subject.

But all poets, schizophrenics, dreamers, hypnotized persons, amnesiacs, self-deceivers, etc. are constanly disabusing us of this illusion. Poets in particular expose the illusion for what it is because they insist on leaving a written record of the splits in their subjectivity. A rather blatant example is the following from Harold Bloom's "Reflections Upon the Path":

(9) $I_{[1]}$ am not $I_{[2]}$, I am not here, here is not here.

Why the subject must endure such a split is not entirely clear. Perhaps he is compelled to imitate or repeat (cf. Freud's "Wiederholungszwang") the original split between the 'absolute' subject and the second subject(s). Perhaps the splitting of the subject is effected in order to isolate incompatible mental impulses from one another (cf. *SE* II, 225-39; XXIII, 275; Fingarette 1974:93). Perhaps, in the case of literary creativity, the relatively modest, non-desiring "sujet zérologique" (Kristeva 1969:195-97, 270-77) has to be made ignorant of the self-aggrandizing, originating subject that seeks immortality in a textual metonym (see below, Chapter VI). Whatever the case, the semiotician can be of assistance by showing *how* the "rejets qui pulvérise le sujet unaire" (Kristeva 1972) are signified. And most commonly the splits are signified by discrepancies involving the category of person.

Consider, for example, the attempt to violate the principle of contradiction in (9). The only way to preserve this basic logical operation in interpreting such an utterance is to posit psychologically different referents for different tokens ('I_1' vs. 'I_2') of the same first person shifter. In other words, the normally *uniform deixis* of the first person pronoun gives way to *non-uniform* or *multiple deixis* of that pronoun. A similar example is the following:

(10)   I had to die to keep from dying,
                                           (schizophrenic patient; Laing 1965:176)

but in this case the two pronouns are not both immediately evident in the surface structure. The "Ichspaltung" is between the subject signified by the overt pronoun in the higher clause "*I* had to die" and

the subject signified by the covert pronoun in the lower clause "*I
keep from dying*". More specifically, the higher clause pronoun de-
notes a split-off subject which was responsible for the patient's
catatonia ("I tried to be dead and grey and motionless"), while the
lower clause pronoun points to a Lacanian true subject, what the
patient called 'the real me', what Laing calls simply the 'self'. The
catatonia of the split-off subject was, in other words, a way of
protecting or defending the true subject. Any equi-noun phrase deletion (Chomsky 1972:57-58) performed by the patient in recounting
her catatonia is only a holdover from normal speech, for the noun
phrases (the pronouns) are hardly 'equi-' on the level of psychological reference. Unable to overcome the automatized deletion process,
the patient attempts to violate the principle of contradiction instead.

Grammatical as well as logical misuse of the category of person is
found in victims of split subjectivity. Consider Rimbaud's famous
declaration to Georges Izambard:

(11)   Les souffrances sont énormes, mais il faut être fort, être
né poète, et je me suis reconnu poète. Ce n'est pas du tout
ma faute. C'est faux de dire: Je pense. On devrait dire: *On
me pense*. Pardon du jeu de mots.
Je est un autre. Tant pis pour le bois qui se trouve
violon, et nargue aux inconscients qui ergotent sur ce qu'ils
ignorent tout à fait! (May, 1871; emphasis added)

Rimbaud could have asserted his identification with the 'autre' by
simply uttering the oxymoron 'je suis un autre'. In such a case there
would have been the usual redundancy between the marking of the
pronoun 'je', $\begin{bmatrix} +\text{person} \\ +\text{personal} \end{bmatrix}$, and the marking of the verb 'suis',
$\begin{bmatrix} +\text{person} \\ +\text{personal} \end{bmatrix}$. As it is, however, he gives us the verb 'est' which is
[−person] and which therefore treats the pronoun as if it too were
unmarked for the category of person In *iconic* fashion the verb fails
to respect the already prior establishment of a thinking subject 'je'
and behaves as if there were some *other* subject, perhaps the 'On' of
the preceding 'On me pense'. Insofar as the signifier of this subject
'fades' behind the signifier 'je', its origin is a Lacanian as well as a
Rimbauldian 'autre'.[2]

The linguistic discrepancy in the Rimbaud example is between two
carriers of the category of person, pronoun and verb. There are
numerous other ways in which the category of person can be set

against itself or some other element for the purpose of signifying an "Ichspaltung". In each case a disturbing psychological effect is produced upon the addressee. The iconic and synaesthetic qualities of a given discrepancy cannot in fact be considered in isolation from one another. The addressee necessarily 'feels' the iconically signified split in the subjectivity of the addresser:

(12)　　　　　　　　　　to love my enemy
　　　　　as I love me — which is quite out of the question!
　　　　　　　　(John Berryman, "Vespers")

(13)　I cannot find me.
　　　Where am I?　　(schizophrenic patient; Laing 1965:171)

(14)　Sometimes going backward toward together I find
　　　Me
　　　　　　　(James Applewhite, "Discardings")

(15)　funny hat with a big feather tied under myhis chin
　　　　　　　(e.e. cummings, "at the head of the street")

(16)　　　　　　　　　　the
　　　romp cries i and the me purrs
　　　　　　　(e.e. cummings, "O the sun")

(17)　who are you, little i

　　　(five or six years old)
　　　peering from some high

　　　window
　　　　　　　(e.e. cummings, "who are you")

In examples (12)-(14) the anaphoric linkage between grammatical subject and object is broken through non-application of a late reflexivization rule (cf. Chomsky 1965:145-46), and it is precisely this grammatical break which makes us 'feel' the psychological rupture. In (15) the poet's split is quite palpably manifested by the indecisive use of oppositely marked pronouns, 'my', which is [+person], and 'his', which is [−person]. In (16) the case-marked form 'me' is played against the case-unmarked form 'i'. In (17) the poet plays instead with the opposition [±personal], 'you' vs. 'i' and, as in (16), 'pseudo-nominalizes' the first person pronoun by slipping it into the nominal slot required after a determiner or adjective. (The latter device has become somewhat hackneyed in Whitman's "the real me", Proust's "un autre moi", Freud's "das Ich", Lacan's "le moi", Potebnja's "ètot ja", etc.). Linguistically such pseudonominalization or lexicalization has the effect of subtracting the category of person from what was originally a pronoun. Psychoanalytically, it provides an iconic/ synaesthetic depersonification of the originating subject of consciousness to the level of 'object'. Which brings us back to Lacan's oxymoron: "it is necessary to find the subject as a lost object" (cf. above, p. 67). The originating or true subject has over time become so isolated from consciousness by repression that it seems to be a lost 'object', and pseudonominalization of the first person pronoun only helps strengthen the sense of that loss. Such pseudonominalization has an even more devastating effect on the 'hereness' and 'nowness' signified by the first person pronoun than does the introduction of marked tense. Thus, for cummings to ask

(18)   who are you, *little i*?

instead of to answer

(19)   you are like me when *I was* little

is to more effectively signal the loss of the childhood subject. Whereas the past tense in (19) makes the present subject of consciousness at least *continuous* with the childhood subject, the pseudonominalization in (18) establishes a *rupture* between the present or speaking subject and the true subject of childhood. The past tense construction merely makes the reader reminisce over time past, while the pseudonominalization captures the speaking subject's real melancholy over an*other* subject irretrievably lost.

But is the originating subject always irretrievably lost? What if the pseudonominalization process is reversed?

(20)   For whatever we lose (like a you or a me)
       it's always ourselves we find in the sea
                     (e.e. cummings, "maggie and milly")

(21)   Ihre [i.e., psychoanalysis'] Absicht ist ja, das Ich zu
       stärken, es vom Über-Ich unabhängiger zu machen, sein
       Wahrnehmungsfeld zu erweitern und seine Organisation
       auszubauen, so dass es sich neue Stücke des Es aneignen
       kann. Wo Es war, soll Ich werden.
                     (Freud 1940 XV:86)

(22)   Là où c'était, peut on dire, là où s'était, voudrions-nous
       faire qu'on entendit, c'est mon devoir que je vienne à être.
                        (Lacan 1966:417-18)

These three utterances share a remarkably similar grammatical
progression: the initial pseudonominalization gives way to a re-
pronominalization of the pronoun. For cummings, 'a you' and 'a me'
become 'ourselves'. For Freud, the more usual 'das Ich' and 'das Es'
become simply 'Ich' and 'Es'. For Lacan, the customary 'le ça'
becomes the elided 'c'' and 'le je' becomes 'je'. In all three utterances
the re-pronominalization is a poetic device which helps us to grasp
the otherwise extremely difficult notion that our locus of subjectivity can after all be reestablished in that place from which it has
been isolated by the barrier of repression, i.e., the device convinces
us that the true subject can be retrieved. At the same time the juxtaposition of (20) with (21) and (22) teaches us that poets and
psychoanalysts, however difficult it may sometimes be for them to
communicate with one another (Laferrière 1973), can nonetheless be
privy to an identical truth.
    Not all instances of discrepant use of the category of person imply
a genuine "Ichspaltung" in the addresser. A discrepancy may only
indicate changing 'point of view' or merely 'shallow' self-deception
(cf. Pears 1974), as in

(23)   If I_1 were you I_2 wouldn't hire me in such a situation,

where 'me' does not get reflexivized to 'myself' because it is not
meant to be coreferential with 'I_2', that is, because the addresser's
momentary identification with the addressee makes the addressee the
reference of 'I_2'. A shift in viewpoint can also take place in soli-
loquistic discourse:

(24)   George Dandin! George Dandin! Vous avez fait une
       sottise. . . . (quoted from Molière by Brown & Gilman
       1960:276; cf. Benveniste 1974:86)

(25)   Durak, ty (You fool!) (cf. Newman 1974)

In such instances the addresser takes the viewpoint of another,
imagined addresser. Yet another example is the scholarly 'we', where
the addresser euphemistically suggests that the addressee stay 'with
him' in the development of an argument:

(26) We have already solved that problem in the preceding
      chapter. (cf. Andreski 1972:193)

None of these examples, however, indicate a true "Ichspaltung" in
the addresser. They are either momentary quips inserted into an
otherwise normal discourse, as in (23)-(25), or else they are merely
clichéd expressions, as in (26). For a discrepancy in the use of the
category of person to truly signify an "Ichspaltung," that discrepancy must be associated with other kinds of linguistic discrepancies,
as in the so-called 'word salad' of a schizophrenic patient or in the
syntactically anomalous poetry of e.e. cummings, or else it must be
associated with some non-linguistic behavioral disturbance, as in
catatonic stupor or fetishism. Thus, although the speaker of (23)
omitted the same grammatical rule (reflexivization) as did the
speaker of (13), one could not say that both omissions signify an
"Ichspaltung". In the case of (23) the slightly inebriated speaker,
who has no history of behavioral disturbances, was merely playing
with the reflexive rule in order to emphasize her identification with
her interlocutor. But in the case of (13) the speaker has a long
history of catatonic and other psychotic episodes.

Sometimes there are no apparent discrepancies in the subject's use
of the category of person, when in fact the discrepancies are dis-
guised because they occur so regularly and systematically. For
example, in the type of paranoia based on latent homosexual impulses, the subject may obsessively repeat a sentence like

(27) *He* persecutes *me*.

According to Freud's famous analysis (*Standard Edition* XII:63), this
sentence really means

(28) *I* love *him*.

In other words, the discrepancy is between a manifest and a latent
statement, rather than within one manifest (surface) statement.

Another example of such latent-to-manifest discrepancy is the
phenomenon of literary inspiration, where the writer unconsciously
projects his own fantasies into some (real or imagined) outside agent
and then 'hears' his fantasies emanate back from that agent. Thus
Shakespeare says

(29) Where art *thou*, Muse, that *thou* forget'st so long
      To speak of that which gives *thee* all *thy* might?
                      (Sonnet C)

instead of

(30) *Where am *I*, that *I* should forget so long
To speak of that which gives *me* all *my* might?

Granted, the writer's projection of his fantasies into a 'muse' can be a very satisfying and aesthetically effective self-deception, but it is still self-deception.[3] It enables the writer to omit first person pronouns from those places in his discourse on *ars poetica* where such pronouns might be harmful to his ego ('ego-distonic'). For example, although Afanasij Fet admits to the embarassing absurdities ("neleposti") in his discourse, he nonetheless blames them on a 'muse', not on himself:

(31)   Moja muza ne lepečet ničego, krome nelepostej.
(My muse babbles nothing but absurdities.)
(from a letter to Ja. Polonskij, 21 November, 1891)

Even when the writer does not bother to personify the source of his inspiration, he still perceives this source as external, as *other*:

(32)   I don't understand the process of imagination – though I know that I am very much at its mercy. I feel that these ideas are floating around me in the air and they pick me to settle upon. The ideas come to me; I don't produce them at will. They come to me in the course of a sort of controlled daydream, a directed reverie. (Joseph Heller)

Such is the disavowal necessary for any literary creativity. The writer hears what Lacan would term a "... discours de l'Autre, où il faut entendre le de au sens du *de* latin (détermination objective): *de Alio in oratione* (achevez: *tua res agitur*) [cf. Horace: *Tua res agitur paries cum proximus ardet*]" (Lacan 1966:814). But if the writer loses direction and control over his reverie, i.e., if the discourse comes to emanate *entirely* from the unconscious split-off portion of the subject, then the originally innocuous disavowal becomes a full-blown schizoid condition. The discourse then produced may be variously described as automatic speaking, word salad, verbigeration, glossolalia, speaking in tongues, etc. (see Brill's discussion of the writing sprees in a schizoid-manic patient who had previously published poetry: 1931:368). In such a situation the poet no longer speaks, but 'is spoken' — to make iconic use of a passive construction. Compare Lacan's expression of the alienation of madness: ". . . le sujet y est parlé plutot qu'il ne parle . . ." (1966:283).

To briefly recapitulate: when the subject suffers from internal splitting, discrepancies involving the category of person are likely to appear in his discourse. These discrepancies may be purely logical, as in attempted violation of the principle of contradiction, but more often they are grammatical, as in the omission of an anaphoric linkage or in pseudonominalization. Not all discrepancies involving the category of person, however, necessarily imply a true splitting of the subject. Moreover, not all splitting of the subject is necessarily revealed by logically and/or grammatically discrepant use of the category of person within the manifest content, for some kinds of person discrepancies consistently occur between the manifest content and the latent or unconscious content of the discourse. In any case, whenever splitting of the subject does occur, the grammatical category of person plays an important role.

NOTES

[1] There are other ways of effecting such a modification, as in

(3) I teach English at X University,
(4) I might do that.

In (3) a generically used verb and in (4) a conditional mood expand upon the 'hereness' and 'nowness' of the pronoun 'I'. In fact, there are probably few utterances like

(5) I am here now,
(6) I am speaking to you this instant.

which do *not* modify the 'hereness' and 'nowness' of the first person shifter.

[2] An opposite (and perhaps more common) process is the 'fading' of the 'je' behind other signifiers, such as 'tu' and 'il'. Kristeva points out many instances of this in Lautréamont's *Chants de Maldoror* (1974:316ff.).

[3] For a detailed biographical discussion of a specific instance of poetic inspiration, see Laferrière 1977b, Exercise I.

VI

The Writing Perversion

Toute l'écriture est de la cochonnerie.

Antonin Artaud

In the beginning, scripture says, was the word. Only after did script appear. True, independent written signs ("semasiographs" – Gelb 1952) existed for some period alongside of spoken language. But when the time came for one system of signs to supplement the other, it was writing that adapted to speaking, not vice-versa. In phylogeny: man produced full writing systems (phonography) in accordance with the dictates of languages already spoken. In ontogeny: the child molds his ABC's onto an already highly developed speaking ability. Perhaps ontogeny is recapitulating phylogeny. Whatever the case, when the written word is viewed diachronically, it is a decidedly derivative or secondary phenomenon.

When viewed synchronically, however, the written word seems to attain a more independent status, as if it were semasiographic again. If I think of a tree, for example, I can say what the phoneticist represents as [čriy] – aloud or silently. Or I can *write* 'tree' – on paper or in my mind. I can, in other words, go automatically from the intended signatum to either its spoken or written signans, without necessarily being aware of any intermediary processes. In particular, the written word 'tree' no longer seems to be accompanied by an intermediary signans [čriy], so automatized are my writing habits. Also, when I see the word 'tree' during 'speed reading', I do not necessarily hear [čriy]. Instead, I progress immediately from the written representation to the sense. When it is a question, then, of reading ordinary prose at an automatized rate, the originally intermediary signans [čriy] is omitted from consciousness. The written word apparently loses its status as signans of a signans.

But when it comes to reading or writing artistic literature, the speech processes which underlie writing are *de*automatized (in the Prague school sense of the term), and the spoken signans suddenly comes back into its own:

> One sigh of real breath — one gentle squeeze,
> Warm as a dove's nest among summer *trees*
>
> (Keats, "Endymion")

Such a rhyme is a distinctly phonological phenomenon, and is not at all hindered by the imperfection of the eye-rhyme 'squeeze~trees'. The reading or writing subject of Keats' lines cannot resist the temptation to *hear*, if only in his mind the word [čriz]. The written word regains its orginal status as mere signans of a signans and re-enters what Hartman calls the "domain of the secondary" (1973:222).

But is there not something offensive about the epithets '*mere* signans of a signans', 'domain of the *secondary*'? Is it not incorrect to say that writing, however matured it may become, is still always the child of speech? We are given to believe that the literary artist, after all, lives his writing, perceives writing as primary, and expects his critic to show equal esteem for the written signans. Just such a critic is Jacques Derrida, who attempts to turn the tables on ("déconstruire") the old notion of (even phonographic) writing as a secondary act: "la parole . . .est déjà en elle-même une écriture": ". . . il n'y a pas de signe linguistique avant l'écriture" (1967b:68, 26).

The basis for Derrida's assertion rests with the idea of *trace*. Any sign, for example, is but a trace of something other than itself and can never be the thing itself. The moment the sign comes into existence (i.e., a word is uttered, a gesture is made, a neuronal message is triggered, etc.), the thing signified is already in the past or in the future. There is no present in Derrida's system, but only a continuous deferment of the present by means of traces. Now, since the written cipher is a trace *par excellence*, it follows by Derrida's peculiarly epitomical reasoning that any sign — spoken, written, or otherwise — is already a kind of written trace or inscription. Thus, for example, every time Robert Frost wrote down 'tree' in his famous poem about birches, he was not only setting ink to paper in order to signify an object in the real world (the conventional notion of writing), but he was also leaving a delayed trace of his immediate and undifferentiated experience of swinging on a birch (Derrida's metaphorical notion of writing). Even an oral recitation of Frost's poem would, by Derrida's theory, be a 'writing' of the poem.

Derrida's scriptive metaphor for the sign can be quite interesting, as when, for instance, it is juxtaposed with Freud's equally scriptive metaphors for the psychical apparatus:

"Bilderschrift" – comparing the interpretation of dreams to the decipherment of ancient Egyptian hieroglyphs,
"Niederschrift" – comparing the coexistence of matching conscious and un-conscious ideas with a double, palimpsestic inscription,
"Wunderblock" – comparing memory to the children's "magic writing pad," from which a written message (=perceptions) may be erased by simply pulling back the outer layer, leaving behind a permanent inscription in the inner layer. (see: "Freud et la scène de l'écriture" in Derrida 1967a:293-340)

Clearly, the scriptive metaphor is not without precedent. But eventually it gets overworked in the hypertrophied Derridian recension. In reading Derrida's works we begin to wonder: is there anything that is *not* a written trace, that is *not* "écriture"? And there is no escaping the metaphor, no way to retreat into the mundane reality of the semiotician who would try to ask, for example, just what the concrete differences between writing and speaking are (cf. Vološinov 1973:111-12).

As for the scriptive bias in Freud that Derrida leans so heavily upon, we must not forget that Freud himself was laboring under the influence of a nineteenth century 'philologistic' (as Vološinov would say) tradition, as is clearly revealed in the paper on "The Philological Interest of Psycho-Analysis (*Standard Edition*, XIII:176-78). Moreover, Freud was apparently ignorant of the advances in linguistics and semiotics being made by Peirce and Saussure. And if Freud, as a good neurologist, were still alive to witness current research in neuro-linguistics (e.g., Jakobson 1974:59-71, Luria 1966, Geschwind 1970), he would most certainly want to abandon his scriptive models for neurolinguistic ones. Consider, for example, the remarkable phenomenon of pure alexia without agraphia:

The visual cortex on the left is destroyed . . . . As a result the patient can perceive written material only in the intact right visual region. For this material to be appreciated *as language* it must be relayed to the *speech* areas on the left side through the splenium, which is the posterior portion of the corpus callosum [a band of fibers uniting the cerebral hemispheres]. As a result of damage to the splenium . ., this transfer cannot take place, and therefore the patient cannot comprehend the *written words whose form he perceives clearly*. (Geschwind 1970:943; emphasis added)

There could hardly be a more convincing demonstration of the dependence of written ciphers upon underlying speech processes. At the same time we are presented with a much more realistic model of the perceptual apparatus (specifically, the portion involved in reading) than the model offered by, say, Freud's "Wunderblock". Not that Freud's model was a bad start. Indeed we may still accept the notion that the perceptual apparatus, including that part involved in reading, consists of ". . . an external protective shield against stimuli whose task it is to diminish the strength of excitations coming in [as in the tough, outer celluloid layer of the "Wunderblock"], and of a surface behind it which receives the stimuli [as in the delicate, waxed paper layer of the "Wunderblock"]" (*Standard Edition* XIX:230). But it makes more sense, now that more is known about cortical functioning than was known in Freud's day, to describe the perceptual apparatus in terms of specific cortical areas than in terms of the layers of a "Wunderblock". Thus the speech areas on the left side should be interpreted as the ultimate receiver of written stimuli, while intervening areas (splenium, right and left visual cortex, optic nerves, eyes) might be interpreted as the collective "protective shield" (Freud) which diminishes and reorganizes the incoming stimuli.

Among contemporary French theoreticians, Derrida is not alone in his scriptive bias. Jacques Lacan, for example, is perhaps best known in non-psychoanalytic circles for his article on the insistence of the *letter* in the unconscious (1966:493-528). As with Derrida's notion of "écriture", Lacan's notion of the letter is metaphorical: "nous désignons par lettre ce support matériel que le discours concret emprunte au langage" (1966:495). There are some, however, who carry the scriptive bias to the point of actually personifying the written text: "le texte que vous écrivez doit me donner la preuve *qu'il me désire.* Cette preuve existe: c'est l'écriture" (*Le plaisir du texte*, 13-14); ". . . the text reads, deciphers, and decodes the subject-reader . . ." (Jean-Michel Pianca 1972:31). Compare the sober, old-fashioned "logocentrisme" (Derrida) of Saussure: "langage et écriture sont deux systèmes de signes distincts; l'unique raison d'être du second est de représenter le premier" (1973 [1915]:45). Clearly, Derrida, Lacan, Barthes, and Pianca have come a long way from Saussure.

But was the trip worth it? Just what is so special about writing? It does not matter here whether the scriptive characterization of any discourse be mildly metaphorical, as in Lacan, intensely anti-logocentric, as in Derrida, or fanatically personifying, as in Barthes and Pianca. Indeed such questions are prompted not only by the peculiarly French fetishization of the written text in recent years, but also by the fact that all literary artists feel compelled to *write* down their inner speech and by the fact that all semioticians need to *write* out their analyses. The latter situation is a particularly strong factor in subliminally encouraging the semiotician to believe that the entities studied, i.e., signs, are in some important sense written. Take a simple monosyllable like [noụ] in English. In addition to the acoustic representation of this syllable (just written) there exist a) a more abstract, i.e., phonemic representation of the syllable, /now/; b) at least two ways of specifying the syllable in the lexicon, $\begin{bmatrix} +\text{interj} \\ +\text{neg} \\ \text{etc.} \end{bmatrix}$

vs. $\begin{bmatrix} +\text{verb} \\ +\text{strong} \\ \text{etc.} \end{bmatrix}$; c) two orthographic representations of the syllable,

'no' vs. 'know'; d) an optional deep structure representation 'neg' that selects the first of the two lexical representations in a generative grammar; and e) a psychoanalytic representation, "Verneinung", which includes the syllable as a repressive device in a utterance like "*No*, it was not my mother that I saw in the dream". With all of these magical looking written representations, then, is it any wonder that semioticians tend to forget that the syllable was originally a *spoken* sign?

But there is a more fundamental reason for the writing bias. Writing is a special or privileged means of signification because it repairs the defect of transience in speech: "les paroles s'envolent, mais les écrits restent." While the spoken word is only for the moment, the written word stays, permitting repetition of the moment, as if indeed by some kind of trickery there were no end (= death) to the subject of the signifying moment. Stated most simply, the written work is the expression of the writing subject's old wish for immortality, and in unguarded lines that subject will tell us of his wish:

> J'écris, je ne veux pas mourir.
> (George Bataille, "Le Roi du Bois")

> Ax! vedaet moj dobryj genij,
> Čto predpočel by ja skorej
> Bessmertiju duši moej
> Bessmertie svoix tvorenij.
> (Aleksandr Puškin, "V al'bom Illičev-
> skomu")

> Ah, my good genius knows
> That I would much prefer
> The immortality of my works
> To the immortality of my soul.
> > (Aleksandr Puškin, "In Illičevskij's al-
> > bum", translated by D. L.)

> Stranger, pause and look;
> > From the dust of ages
> Lift this little book,
> > Turn the tattered pages,
> Read me, do not let me die!
> > (Edna St. Vincent Millay, "The Poet and
> > His Book")

But what precisely is the trick whereby the writer's subjectivity is shifted from his mortal self into the allegedly immortal text? In what sense are we justified in saying that writing is ". . . a consuming of the self . . . in order to escape that annihilation of the self that is the inevitable outcome of physical generation" (Irwin 1975:159)? It is the duty of the semiotician not to be taken in by the trick, not to collaborate with the writer's fetishization of writing, but to lay bare the signifying processes behind the trick.

The trick is metonymy, i.e., the rhetorical device whereby one item is made to stand for (re-present) a second, spatiotemporally contiguous item (I adhere to Jakobson's broader and more traditional notion of metonymy, which includes synecdoche, as opposed to the narrower notion of metonymy recently proposed by "le groupe μ": Jakobson and Halle 1956; Dubois *et al.* 1970). The phrase "made to stand for" is crucial here because a metonymic representation cannot occur without some factor that temporarily *distorts* the original relationship of mere contiguity into one of similarity, i.e., identity. Thus when the high school teacher instructs the student

> Open your Shakespeare,

instead of

> Open your book which contains the works that were writ-
> ten many years ago by Shakespeare,

the original spatiotemporal contiguity between "Shakespeare" (the

man who lived and died several centuries ago) and "the book which
contains the works that were written by Shakespeare" is transformed
into a similarity: "Shakespeare" at the performative instant *is* "the
book which etc. etc.". True, from the teacher's viewpoint the
metonymic equation of the man with the book is but an energy-
saving, economic device, as in the waiter's shortcut question

> Are you the sauerkraut?,

instead of

> Are you the person who ordered the sauerkraut?

But from Shakespeare's point of view the teacher's energy-saver signals fulfillment of a wish:

> . . . Death to me subscribes
> Since, spite of him, I'll live in this poor rime.
> (Sonnet CVII)

It is as if Shakespeare were alive and well in his "poor rime". He is of
course neither well nor alive, but quite dead — a truism which no
doubt grates on our natural tendency to identify with his wish for
immortality. We are all too anxious to embrace the beautiful wish
and to renounce understanding, i.e., understanding of death:

> Der Tod, wenn wir jene Unwirklichkeit so nenne wollen,
> ist das Fruchtbarste, und das Tote festzuhalten, das, was
> die grösste Kraft erfordert. *Die kraftlose Schönheit hasst
> den Verstand*, weil er ihr dies zumutet, was sie nicht ver-
> mag. Aber nicht das Leben, das sich vor dem Tode scheut
> und von der Verwüstung rein bewahrt, sondern das ihn
> erträgt, und in ihm sich erhält, ist das Leben des Geistes.
> (Hegel 1937 [1807]:29, emphasis added)

Every literary artist hopes that we will be seduced by the "Schön-
heit" he proffers us, that we will fail to apply our "Verstand" to his
magical thinking. In short, he believes we will resurrect him into
being by merely reading his text:

> Puisque tu me lis, cher lecteur, donc je suis . . . .
> (Francis Ponge, *Pour un Malherbe*)

But such reasoning is as gratuitous as the Cartesian *Cogito* itself. The scriptive fixation that lurks in Ponge's reasoning may be quickly discerned if the Lacanian version of the *Cogito* is also brought to bear upon our argument:

> Cogito, ergo sum, *ubi* cogito, *ibi* sum.
> (Lacan 1966:516)

We then obtain a hybrid statement that nicely defines the imputed locus of the literary artist's subjectivity:

> Since you read me, dear reader, therefore I am;
> where you read me, there I am, i.e., *in the written*
> *text* ("in this poor rime").

The falsehood of such magical, metonymic reasoning is made evident not only by the real mortality of the writing subject, but also by the morbid qualities which the metonym itself acquires. Thus we have such expressions as: "the dead letter", "dead languages", "linguistic cadavers", "the letter killeth", etc. Writing, in other words, is bound to get contaminated by the unspeakable phenomenon against which it is originally a reaction.

Although writing cannot accomplish immortality, it can and does accomplish other, more modest goals. It can bring the writer fame and fortune in his own lifetime. It can become the hyperdeveloped means of communication with the outside world, as in hysterical aphonia (see Freud's experience with Dora, *Standard Edition* VII). Or, it can express things that are simply difficult to say aloud:

> Speech found the ear, for all the evil sound,
> But the dark italics it could not propound.
> (Wallace Stevens, "Esthétique du Mal")
> ... l'écriture commence là où la parole devient impossible ... (Roland Barthes 1971:3)

Two things in particular allow writing to overcome the difficulties of speaking. First, writing is *silent*, i.e., it imitates unspeakability by repressing speech while at the same time it also manages to signify the unspeakable with written ciphers (the writer has his cake and eats it too). Second, writing is *corrigible*. When a slip of the pen does irrupt from the timeless unconscious into the temporal discourse, it can be quickly erased and corrected, never to appear in the final draft, never to require an embarassing oral apology from the writer. The writer can go on safely with his writing despite, as Kafka says, all the wrong sentences which curl like snakes around the point of the pen. A slip of the tongue, on the other hand, cannot be taken back: "Slovo ne vorobej, vyletit – ne ipojmaeš'" ("the word is no sparrow – once it flies off, you won't catch it"). Thus there are other enticements to writing besides the trick of scriptive metonymy.

Freud called his invention the "speaking cure". But whereas speaking cures, writing is but a palliative therapy (H. D. recognized this during her sessions with Freud). Writing is too close to mortality to cure. Let us quote from the diary of D. Kuznetzov:

A lover departs and I must write – she may run away or she may be sent away – no difference, for in either case I have to work through the pain of her absence. First comes the obsession with little things –
> "her sometime eyes,"
> "her any gesture in every passer-by,"
> "the hollow of my elbow where she lay her tangled hair," etc. etc.
– all of the spicy little signals that we romantics live by, that reduce us to despicable whimpering over time irretrievably past. But these signals of her absence grow to monstrous proportions in my memory and I can no longer bear them, I must find a friend and talk them out of my system, or I must find paper and write them out of my system. The first alternative is never satisfactory, for a friend talks back, he forces me to talk with him instead of with myself. Yes I know speaking is an easier and more natural protest against her absence. Screaming at someone in fact would probably be the best protest. A minimal effort. You just let go. Even throw in a few primal screams.

But writing is another matter. There is no conversation except the one inside, which is false, i.e. which is between me and the make-believe presence of her, whose absence I protest. I know that sooner or later I shall become reconciled with her absence, that indeed I shall find another woman with whom I can strike up a goodbye. In the meantime it is precisely the absence that I thrive on, that I obsessively repeat in preparation for the ultimate absence, the absence of myself from the world.

This description of the genesis of one kind of love lyric may now be paraphrased into five stages within the poet's cyclically unhappy consciousness:

1) *Readying*: the poet admits to himself (as did Freud in *Traumdeutung*) that no one is irreplaceable, and it becomes compellingly clear that his readiness is all.

2) *Loving*: the readied poet fixates upon an object in the external world, introjects that object *into* the position of a previously lost object.

3) *Parting*: the poet loses the object in the external world, but still possesses the introjected object.

4) *Mourning*: the poet gets moody and melancholic, i.e., he hypercathects the metonymic representations of the lost object ("her sometime eyes", "her tangled hair", etc.).

5) *Writing*: the poet writes the introjected object *out* of his system, i.e. he deposits the hypercathected metonyms of the object into a written text.

1) *Readying*: the poet admits to himself that . . ., etc. etc.

Note the double role which metonymy plays in this sequence: on the one hand the resulting poem is itself the magical metonym for the poet (scriptive metonymy), while on the other hand the text contains the hypercathected metonyms of the object he is trying to 'cast out' of himself. In a single act of writing, then, two kinds of metonymic representations are being deposited in the external world. Whereas the aim of the scriptive metonym is to establish the poet's immortal *presence* in the world, the aim of the ex-lover's metonyms is to establish her *absence* in the poet. The combined effect of these two metonymic transfers of subjectivity is an illusion that the poem is a more valid locus of subjectivity than the poet, is somehow more of a person than is the poet.

Closely bound up with scriptive metonymy, then, is the rhetorical process of personification. But the personification itself engenders an opposite: even as the writer is forcibly displacing his subjectivity into his text, so too he is also effacing himself before his reader, attempting to *de*-personify himself. This "travail du *je* vers l'impersonnel", as Meschonnic calls it, is a very necessary and pleasurable trope, as necessary and as pleasurable as the textual personification with which it is bound. It certainly appeals to the romantic stereotype of the writer as inspired mouthpiece of his muse, as a passive subject who does not speak but who is "spoken." In point of fact, however, there is no ego bigger than the writer's ego, there is no subject more active and self-aggrandizing than the writing subject. And this subject takes great delight in making an apparent zero of himself, in effect saying: "Look, I am not really myself when I write, I am inspired by a muse, I lose control, I lose myself in my writing, etc., etc.", which the typical Parisian-style 'structuralist' obligingly interprets as: "Look, he is not really himself when he writes, he relinquishes control to the internal demands of the growing text, his subjectivity can no longer be separated from the text, in fact his subjectivity must be *in the text* ("dans le texte")." But these are half-truths because the writer is himself split in half, is suffering from a fundamental

"Ichspaltung" (Freud; cf. above, Chapter V). The first half, the half which is so often ignored, is the subject of a *desire* to write. This subject continues to exist during the metonymic bringing-into-the-world of the text (cf. Lacan 1966:528, for his equation of metonymy with desire). Sometimes this originating subject may actually reveal himself, as when the persona of a lyric poem blatantly declares a wish for immortality. But usually the originating subject cannot be directly retrieved from the text. He is *outside* the text, busily seeing to it that the text gets written and gets readable. If this subject did not continue to exist, if he were to disappear and become a zero, as some would have us believe (cf. Kristeva's "sujet zérologique"), then the desire to bring the text into the world would also disappear, and zero desire means zero text.

The second half of the writing subject is absolute. He is Hegel's subject of "absolutes Wissen", Lacan's "sujet vrai". This more mystical subject, which we may interchangeably describe as a zero or as an infinity, is not to be confused with the originating subject, the subject who initially desired to bring the text into the world. Desire is irrelevant to the absolute subject, though he does not mind occasionally being pressed into the service of the originating subject (the very pronominalization of the absolute subject with a 'he' instead of an 'it' is an example). The absolute subject plays with, disorients, and sometimes even takes the liberty of annihilating the grounds of the originating subject's existence. But the originating subject persistently returns to elaborate a new position from which he can act out his desire. The originating subject never gives in to the surrounding absolute void. He cannot conceive of his own destruction.

The interplay of originating vs. absolute subject is difficult to describe. Paradoxes and contradictions arise. Part of the problem concerns pronouns. The writer needs at least two first person singular pronouns in order to differentiate the two subjects of the "Ichspaltung" he suffers, whereas his language provides only one such pronoun. Consider, for example, the marvelous contradictions in the following passage by Roger Laporte (who does *not* fall under the rubric of 'typical Parisian 'structuralist''):

... celui qui dit je, acteur certes indispensable au jeu littéraire, est en même temps si étranger à ce qui se joue qu'il peut seulement, de l'extérieur, commenter la partie, désigner du doigt les actions majeures qu'il ne voit point, car elles se déroulent sur une autre scène [cf. Freud's "ein anderer Schauplatz"], hors de la portée de sa vue, ou plutôt il y a une seule scène qui fascine le spectateur, ou mieux le récitant, à jamais mal placé, car le coeur secret du drame, qui se déroule sous ses yeux, échappe a tout spectacle. Celui qui dit je, encore qu'il tienne un rôle ambigu, incessible et provisoire d'instrumental, ne constitue donc pas le sujet reel du verbe écrire, mais, toujours en retard, il n'occupe, dans l'économie de l'écriture, qu'une place marginale, excentrée, ou, pour mieux dire, toujours reculée aussi bien dans l'espace que dans le temps. Ecrire est un verbe neutre que l'on pourrait accompagner, comme tout verbe impersonnel, d'un neutre sujet: il, ne représentant aucun agent. Ce verbe est-il intransitif ou pronominal réfléchi? Faut-il dire: il écrit, ou bien: il s'écrit? (1970:143)

In effect 'je' is opposed to 'il' as originating subject to absolute subject. But 'il' does not capture the "first person-ness" sensed in the absolute subject. Another alternative is that proposed by Roland Barthes:

... if language followed literature — which, for once perhaps, has the lead — I would say that we should no longer say today "j'ai écrit" but, rather, "je suis écrit", just as we say "je suis né, il est mort, elle est éclose". (1970:143)

But this formulation fails to name the absolute subject even as the originating subject is overpowered by the absolute subject. What western languages need are pairs of pronominal shifters (not merely nouns) that succeed in designating both halves of the writer's "Ichspaltung" while at the same time maintaining the 'first person-ness' of each half: e.g., 'I_1' vs 'I_2', or 'je$_1$' vs. 'je$_2$'. Writing might seem less perverse if pronouns were more accommodating. Compare the strangeness of the schizophrenic utterance "I had to die in order to keep from dying" (one of R. D. Laing's patients): the utterance would not be such a blatant attempt to violate the principle of contradiction if two first person pronouns had been available to the patient, one to designate the subject that went catatonic and one to designate the subject that was saved by the catatonia (see above, 68).

But to return to the writing perversion. The effect of the literary artist's metonymic trickery is to make the originating subject fade behind a smokescreen of signifiers. We do not necessarily perceive the originating subject because we were not present during the genesis of the work, during those moments when the originating subject was overpowered ('inspired') by a barrage of signifiers emitted by the absolute subject. After this process is finished the originating subject cannot take much credit for what has happened, though he can truly declare that he has experienced pleasure and pain, that he has been intimately involved in the genesis of the text. In the ideal situation he is modest. When first reading *War and Peace*, for example, we are so taken with the characterizations of Pierre, Natasha, Andrej, etc., that

Tolstoj himself seems to disappear in a most beautiful way. But the disappearance wasn't beautiful while it was happening. It was agonizing. It was ugly. It was pain and a perverse pleasure as well. Incidentally, this conception of writing as *pain*, a conception which both literary artists and critics freely discussed during the Romantic period, and which nowadays is considered unmentionable in most quarters, is probably due for a revival. But, fashionable or unfashionable, the conception was provoked by a truth. We need only examine Tolstoj's diaries, for example, to be convinced that he suffered during the writing of *War and Peace*. Tolstoj had to *part* with a host of interacting subjectivities (=characters), he had to deposit his novel in the world. This formation of a discontinuity between the originating subject and the metonymic shard of subjectivity known as the text can be endured by only the hardiest and most expansive subjects. The writing subject gets so puffed up with all his lesser loci of subjectivity that finally he has to 'burst', to tear himself forever from the metonym he deposits. The negative qualities of such a deposition — ugliness, pain, risk, embarrassment — were evident enough to Tolstoj to make him later condemn as sinful precisely those works (including *War and Peace*) which represented the greatest expansions of his subjectivity and the most artful concealments of the originating subject. The negative qualities of literary deposition were evident enough to Puškin to make him refer to his work as his *drjan'* ('load of rubbish'). And Shakespeare felt obliged to say

> For I am sham'd by that which I bring forth,
> And so should you, to love things nothing worth.
> (Sonnet LXXII)

For us, the writer's feelings of disgust toward his own writing may seem somewhat bizarre. But there is a relatively straightforward psychoanalytic basis for such feelings. We need only think of some of the standard representations which writing receives from the writer. First, writing may be thought of as fecal: "can it be they [Aristotle, Epicurus, and other philosophers] all shat syllogisms, that have nor stench nor stain?", moans Ebenezer Cooke as he is about to wipe his bum with the as yet unwritten pages of his Maryland epic (Barth, *The Sot Weed Factor*). Second, writing may be thought of as phallic: an old meaning of 'castrate' is to expurgate a text (cf. Irwin's discussion of writing as 'self-castration' 1975:171). Third, writing may be thought of as a child: Zamjatin reacts to the budding Soviet censorship with a declaration that his only children are his books ("Moi deti — moi knigi; drugix u menja net"; compare also the 'post-partum depression' a writer often endures after completing a work).

These various representations of writing lead us directly to a universal of the unconscious, to Freud's equation of three basic metonyms of the body, "faeces = penis = baby" (*Standard Edition* XVII:127-33), and suggest that we expand Freud's equation with a fourth term: faeces = penis = baby = text. The textual metonym is capable of occasionally being represented by the more basic body metonyms in even the conscious discourse of the writer. Most of the time, however, it is probably the other way around: the more basic body metonyms are being represented by the textual metonym in the writer's unconscious, in the discourse from the Other (Lacan's "discours de l'Autre"). And if we consider how repulsive is the disassociation of any one of the basic body metonyms from any subject, perhaps we have at least some explanation for the pain and ugliness often connected with deposition of the textual metonym in the world: defecation = castration = parturition = writing. This latter equation is not intended to annihilate such notions as "*belles* lettres" or "*plaisir* du text", but puts such notions into a perspective that has been missing for too long.

At this point we may begin to wonder how anyone would ever dare to set pen to paper, if writing has so many negative qualities. In fact writers *are* in the minority, i.e., there are relatively few individuals who practice the writing perversion, who deviate from the norm of being satisfied with speech as the predominant means of expression. These few individuals either suppress any awareness that writing is perverse (what inferior writers do), or they continually strive to make written language approximate spoken language (what superior writers do). The approximation can never be perfect, that is, writing approaches speech only asymptotically. But still, the best writing does not strike us as written. Writing which re-verts as much as possible to the natural, spoken language is the least per-verse. Osip Mandel'štam, the greatest Russian poet since Puškin, was particularly adamant on this point:

U menja net rukopisej, net zapisnyx knižek, net arxivov. U menja net počerka, potomu čto ja nikogda ne pišy. Ja odin v Rossii rabotaju s golosu, a vokrug gustopsovaja svoloč' pišet. Kakoj ja k čërtu pisatel'! Pošli von, duraki! (*Četvertaja proza*)

I have no manuscripts, no notebooks, no archives. I have no handwriting because I never write. I alone in Russia work from the voice, and all around me the abominable riff-raff writes. What the hell kind of a writer am I? Get out of here you fools! (*Fourth Prose*)

This (ironically) printed harrangue is illustrated by an incident from real life:

Wierdo? Of course he was a wierdo. Once, for example, he kicked out a young poet who had come up to complain about not getting published. The embarrassed young man was going down the stairs as Osip yelled at him from the top stair: "Did André Chénier publish? Did Sappho publish? Did Christ publish?" (Anna Axmatova, *Sočinenija* II:187)

We may paraphrase Mandel'štam's wisdom thus:

I prefer not to think of myself as a writer. I am a speaker. Writing would, were I not careful, pervert my speaking. Therefore, *where my speaking was, there my writing shall be.*

Such a paraphrase is meant to be a special corollary to Freud's well known general postulate: "Wo Es war, soll Ich werden." The writer would do well to recall the corollary on days when he is finding it difficult to live with the perversion he practices.

Bibliography

Andreski, Stanislav
   1972   *Social Sciences as Sorcery*. New York: St. Martin's Press.
Ashbery, John
   1975   *Self-Portrait in a Convex Mirror*. New York: Viking.
Auerbach, Erich
   1953   *Mimesis*, trans. Willard R. Trask. Princeton, N.J.: Princeton University Press.
Axmatova, Anna
   1967- *Sočinenija*. 2 vols. Munich: Inter-Language Literary Associates.
   68
Bailey, James
   1968   "The Basic Structural Characteristics of Russian Literary Meters", *Studies Presented to Professor Roman Jakobson by His Students*, 17-38. Cambridge: Slavica Publishers.
Bailey, Richard
   1977   "Maxwell's Demon and the Muse", *Dispositio* I, No. 3, 293-301.
Bär, Eugen
   1974   "Understanding Lacan", *Psychoanalysis and Contemporary Science: An Annual of Integrative and Interdisciplinary Studies*, 473-544. New York: IUP.
Barthes, Roland
   1970   "To Write: An Intransitive Verb?", *The Structuralist Controversy, the Languages of Criticism and the Sciences of Man*, ed. R. Macksey and E. Donato, 134-45. Baltimore: Johns Hopkins Press.
   1971   "Ecrivains, Intellectuels, Professeurs", *Tel Quel* 47:1-18.
   1973   *Le plaisir du texte*. Paris: Seuil.
Bass, Alan
   1974   "'Literature'/Literature", *Velocities of Change*, ed. Richard Macksey, 341-53. Baltimore: Johns Hopkins Press.
Bateson, Gregory
   1968   "Redundancy and Coding", *Animal Communication: Techniques of Study and Results of Research*, ed. Thomas A. Sebeok, 614-26. Bloomington: Indiana University Press.

Benveniste, Émile
1966, *Problèmes de linguistique générale*. 2 vols. Paris: Gallimard.
1974
Bercovitch, Sacvan
1968   "Literature and the Repetition Compulsion", *College English* 29,
       607-15.
Blanchot, Maurice
1955 *L'espace littéraire*. Paris: Gallimard.
Bloom, Harold
1973 *The Anxiety of Influence: A Theory of Poetry*. New York: Oxford
     University Press.
Brecht, Richard
1974   "Deixis in Embedded Structures", *Foundations of Language* 11,
       489-518.
Brill, A. A.
1931   "Poetry as an Oral Outlet", *The Psychoanalytic Review* 18, 357-78.
Brown, Norman O.
1966 *Love's Body*. New York: Vintage.
Brown, Roger, and Albert Gilman
1960   "The Pronouns of Power and Solidarity", *Style in Language*, ed. Th.
       A. Sebeok, 253-76. Cambridge: MIT Press.
Buchler, Justus
1940 *The Philosophy of Peirce: Selected Writings*. New York: Harcourt
     Brace.
Chatman, Seymour
1965 *A Theory of Meter*. The Hague: Mouton.
Cherry, Colin
1957 *On Human Communication*. Cambridge, New York, London: MIT
     Press, John Wiley, Chapman & Hall.
Chomsky, Noam
1965 *Aspects of the Theory of Syntax*. Cambridge: MIT Press.
1972 *Language and Mind*. New York: Harcourt Brace Jovanovich.
Derrida, Jacques
1967a *L'écriture et la différence*. Paris: Seuil.
1967b *De la grammatologie*. Paris: Editions de minuit.
Dubois, J. et al. ("le groupe μ")
1970 *Rhétorique générale*. Paris: Larousse.
Eco, Umberto
1972   "Introduction to a Semiotics of Iconic Signs", *Versus* 2/1, 1-15.
1976 *A Theory of Semiotics*. Bloomington: Indiana University Press.
Eliot, T. S.
1971 *The Complete Poems and Plays, 1909-1950*. New York: Harcourt,
     Brace and World.
Empson, William
1966   [1930] *Seven Types of Ambiguity*. New York: New Directions.
Fairley, Irene
1975 *E. E. Cummings and Ungrammar*. New York: Watermill.
Fenichel, Otto
1936   "Die symbolische Gleichung: Mädchen = Phallus", *Internat. Zeitschr.
       für Psychoanalyse* 22, 199-214.

Ferenczi, Sandor
1952 [1913] *First Contributions to Psycho-Analysis*. London: Hogarth.
1972 [orig. 1919-23] *Schriften zur Psychoanalyse*. Frankfurt: S. Fischer.
Filmore, Charles
1973 "May We Come In?", *Semiotica* 9, 97-116.
Fingarette, Herbert
1974 "Self-Deception and 'Splitting of the Ego'", *Freud: A Collection of Critical Essays*, ed. Richard Wollheim, 80-96. New York: Doubleday.
Flügel, J. C.
1924 "Polyphallic Symbolism and the Castration Complex", *International Journal of Psycho-Analysis* 5, 155-96.
Fokkema, D. W.
1976 "Continuity and Change in Russian Formalism, Czech Structuralism, and Soviet Semiotics", *PTL* 1, 153-96.
Fónagy, Ivan
1970 "Les bases pulsionelles de la phonation", *Revue française de psychanalyse* 34, 101-36.
Fraisse, Paul
1956 *Les structures rythmiques*. Louvain: Publications universitaires.
1963 *The Psychology of Time*, trans. Jennifer Leith. New York: Harper & Row.
Frazer, James George
1951 *The Golden Bough*, abridged one volume edition. New York: Macmillan.
Freud, Sigmund
1940- *Gesammelte Werke*. 18 vols. London: Imago.
1952
1953- *Standard Edition of the Complete Psychological Works of Sigmund*
1965 *Freud*, trans. under direction of J. Strachey. 24 vols. London: Hogarth Press.
Gelb, I. J.
1952 *A Study of Writing: The Foundations of Grammatology*. Chicago: University of Chicago Press.
Geschwind, N.
1970 "The Organization of Language and the Brain", *Science* 170, 940-44.
Gogol, Nikolai
1964 [1842] *Dead Souls*, trans. Helen Michailoff. New York: Washington Square Press.
Graves, Robert
1966 *Collected Poems*. Garden City: Doubleday Anchor.
Halle, Morris and Samuel Jay Keyser
1971 *English Stress – Its Form, Its Growth, and Its Role in Verse*. New York: Harper and Row.
Harris, James
1751 *Hermes: or a Philosophical Inquiry Concerning Language and Universal Grammar*. London: Woodfall.
Hartman, Geoffrey
1973 "The Interpreter: A Self-Analysis", *New Literary History* 4, 213-27.
Hegel, G. W. F.
1937 [1807] *Phänomenologie des Geistes*. Leipzig: Felix Meiner.

Heidegger, Martin
   1962   *Being and Time*, trans. J. MacQuarrie and E. Robinson. London: SCM
          Press.
Holland, Norman
   1968   *The Dynamics of Literary Response*. New York: Oxford University
          Press.
Huxley, Renira
   1970   "The Development of the Correct Use of Subject Personal Pronouns
          in Two Children", *Advances in Psycholinguistics*, ed. Giovanni B.
          Flores d'Arcais and Willem J. M. Levelt, 141-65. New York: American
          Elsevier.
Irwin, John
   1975   *Doubling and Incest/Repetition and Revenge: A Speculative Reading
          of Faulkner*. Baltimore: Johns Hopkins University Press.
Jakobson, Roman
   1960a "Linguistics and Poetics", *Style in Language*, ed. T. A. Sebeok, 350-77.
          Cambridge: MIT Press.
   1960b "Why 'Mama' and 'Papa'?", *Perspectives in Psychological Theory*, ed.
          Bernard Kaplan, Seymour Wapner, 124-33. New York: IUP.
   1961   "Poèzija grammatiki i grammatika poèzii", *Poetics, Poetyka, Poètika*
          (Warsaw), 397-417.
   1965   "Quest for the Essence of Language", *Diogenes* 51, 21-37.
   1966a "Grammatical Parallelism and Its Russian Facet", *Language* 42/2,
          399-429.
   1966b "'Devuška pela': Nabljudenija nad jazykovym stroem stansov Alek-
          sandra Bloka", *Orbis Scriptus, Dmitrij Tschižewskij, zum 70.
          Geburtstag*, 385-401. München: Wilhelm Fink.
   1970a "On the Verbal Art of William Blake and Other Poet-Painters", *Lin-
          guistic Inquiry* 1, 3-23.
   1970b "Language in Relation to Other Communication Systems", *Linguaggi
          nella società e nella tecnica*, 3-16. Milan: Edizioni di Comunità.
   1970c "The Modular Design of Chinese Regulated Verse", *Exchanges et
          communications, mélanges offerts à Claude Lévi-Strauss à l'occasion
          de son 60ème anniversaire*, réunis par Jean Pouillon et Pierre Maranda,
          597-605. The Hague: Mouton.
   1971a "Stixi skul'ptura", introduction in: Mirtala Kardinalovskaja, *Stixi*, 3-4.
          Madrid: Ediciones Castille.
   1971b *Selected Writings*, Vol. 2. The Hague: Mouton.
   1973   *Questions de poétique*. Paris: Seuil.
   1974   *Main Trends in the Science of Language*. New York: Harper & Row.
Jakobson, Roman, and Morris Halle
   1956   *Fundamentals of Language*. The Hague: Mouton.
Jespersen, Otto
   1949   *Language: Its Nature, Development and Origin*. New York: Macmillan.
Joly, André
   1973   "Sur le système de la personne", *Revue des langues Romanes* 80,
          3-56.
Jones, Ernest
   1913   *Papers on Psycho-Analysis*. London: Baillière.

Jones, Richard
   1970   *The New Psychology of Dreaming*. New York: Grune & Stratton.
Jung, C. G.
   1959   *Mandala Symbolism*, trans. R. F. C. Hull. Princeton: Princeton University Press.
Kondratov, A. M.
   1969   (1963) "Information Theory and Poetics: The Entropy of Russian Speech Rhythm", *Statistics and Style*, ed. L. Doležel and R. Bailey, 113-21. New York: American Elsevier.
Kris, Ernst
   1952   *Psychoanalytic Explorations in Art*. New York: International Universities Press.
Kristeva, Julia
   1969   Σημειωτκή: *Recherches pour une sémanalyse*. Paris: Seuil.
   1972   "Le sujet en procès", *Tel Quel* 52, 12-30.
   1974   *La révolution du langage poétique*. Paris: Seuil.
Lacan, Jacques
   1966   *Ecrits*. Paris: Seuil.
   1970   "Of Structure as an Inmixing of an Otherness Prerequisite to any Subject Whatsoever", *The Structuralist Controversy, the Languages of Criticism and the Sciences of Man*, ed. R. Macksey and E. Donato, 186-95. Baltimore: Johns Hopkins Press.
Laferrière, Daniel
   1972   "Similarity and Contiguity Processes in the Dream Work", *Sub-Stance* 3, 39-52.
   1973   "The Poet and His Analyst", *Sub-Stance* 7, 149-53.
   1974   "Automorphic Structures in the Poem's Grammatical Space", *Semiotica* 10, 333-50.
   1976a   "Potebnja, Šklovskij, and the Familiarity/Strangeness Paradox", *Russian Literature* 4, 175-98.
   1976b   "The Writing Perversion", *Semiotica* 18/3, 217-33.
   1977a   "The Subject and Discrepant Use of the Category of Person", *Versus* 14, 93-104.
   1977b   *Five Russian Poems: Exercises in a Theory of Poetry*. Englewood, N.J.: Trans-World.
   1977c   "Free and Non-Free Verse", *Language and Style* 10, 79-85.
   1978a   "The Teleology of Russian Syllabo-Tonic Rhythm", to appear in *Russian Literature*.
   1978b   "Contiguity Breeds Similarity", to appear in the proceedings of the first meeting of the Semiotic Society of America.
Laing, R. D.
   1965   *The Divided Self*. Baltimore: Penguin.
Laporte, Roger
   1970   *Fugue*. Paris: Gallimard.
Lashley, K. S.
   1961   "The Problem of Serial-Order in Behavior", *Psycholinguistics: A Book of Readings*, ed. Sol Saporta, 180-98. New York: Holt, Rinehart and Winston.
Lehner, Joseph
   1966   *A Short Course in Automorphic Functions*. New York: Holt, Rinehart and Winston.

Lerner, Arthur
    1973   "Poetry Therapy", *American Journal of Nursing* 73, 1336-38.
    1976   "Editorial: A Look at Poetry Therapy", *Art Psychotherapy* 3, i-ii.
Loewenberg, Ina
    1975   "Identifying Metaphors", *Foundations of Language* 12, 315-38.
Lotman, Jurij
    1968   *Lekcii po struktural'noj poètika*. Providence: Brown University
            Slavic Reprints.
    1971   *Struktura xudožestvennogo teksta*. Providence: Brown University
            Slavic Reprints.
Luria, A. R.
    1966a   *Higher Cortical Functions in Man*, trans. Basil Haigh. New York: Basic
            Books.
    1966b   *Human Brain and Psychological Processes*, trans. Basil Haigh. New
            York: Basic Books.
McCanles, Michael
    1975   "All Discourse Aspires to the Analytic Proposition" (ms.), delivered at
            1975 MLA meeting, San Francisco.
Meschonnic, Henri
    1973   *Pour la poétique II*. Paris: Gallimard.
    1975   *Le signe et le poème*. Paris: Gallimard.
Moles, Abraham
    1966   [1958] *Information Theory and Esthetic Perception*, trans. Joel
            Cohen. Urbana: University of Illinois Press.
Morris, Charles W.
    1946   *Signs, Language and Behavior*. New York: George Braziller.
Musil, Robert
    1965   [1930] *The Man Without Qualities*, trans. Eithne Wilkins and Ernst
            Kaiser. New York: Capricorn.
Newman, Lawrence
    1974   "Remarks on the Category of Person in Russian", paper delivered at
            Soviet-American Conference on Russian Language, M.I.T.
Pears, David
    1974   "Freud, Sartre and Self-Deception", *Freud: A Collection of Critical
            Essays*, ed. Richard Wollheim, 97-112. New York: Doubleday.
Peirce, Charles Sanders
    1965-   *Collected Papers of Charles Sanders Peirce*, eds. Charles Hartshorne,
      66   Paul Weiss, and Arthur W. Burks. 8 vols. Cambridge: Harvard Uni-
            versity Press.
Perelman, Ch., and L. Olbrechts-Tyteca
    1969   [1958] *The New Rhetoric, A Treatise on Argumentation*, trans. John
            Wilkinson and Purcell Weaver. Notre Dame: University of Notre Dame
            Press.
Piaget, Jean
    1962   *Play, Dreams and Imitation in Childhood*, trans. C. Gattegno and
            F. M. Hodgson. New York: Norton.
Pianca, Jean Michel
    1972   "The Reading of the Text", *Sub-Stance* 3, 31-38.

Poe, Edgar Allan
1904 "The Rationale of Verse", *The Works of Edgar Allan Poe*. New York: Funk and Wagnalls. [Article first published in 1843].

Posner, Roland
1976 "Poetic Communication vs. Literary Language or: The Linguistic Fallacy in Poetics", *PTL* 1, 1-10.

Pribram, K.
1962 "The Neuropsychology of Sigmund Freud", *Experimental Foundations of Clinical Psychology*, ed. Arthur Bachrach, 442-68. New York: Basic Books.

Quine, Willard Van Orman
1960 *Word and Object*. Cambridge: MIT Press.

Radlov, E. L.
1908 *Pis'ma Vl. Solov'ëva*. St. Petersburg.

Rank, Otto
1929 *The Trauma of Birth*. New York: Harcourt Brace.

Revzin, I. I.
1962 "Soveščanie v g. Gor'kom, posvjaščennoe primeneniju matematičeskix metodov k izučeniju jazyka xudožestvennoj literatury", *Strukturno-tipologičeskie issledovanija*, ed. T. N. Mološnaja, 285-93. Moscow.

Rewar, Walter
1976 "Tartu Semiotics", *Bulletin of Literary Semiotics* 3, 1-16.

Ricoeur, Paul
1975 *La métaphore vive*. Paris: Seuil.

Rosolato, Guy
1974 "L'oscillation métaphoro-métonymique", *Topique* 13, 75-99.

De Saussure, Ferdinand
1973 [1915] *Cours de linguistique générale*. Paris: Payot.

Schneiderman, Stuart
1974 "The Saying of Hamlet", *Sub-Stance* 8, 77-88.

Sebeok, Thomas A.
1975 "The Semiotic Web: A Chronicle of Prejudices", *Bulletin of Literary Semiotics* 2, 1-62.
1976 "Iconicity", *Modern Language Notes* 91, 1427-56.

Shands, Harley
1971 *The War with Words: Structure and Transcendence*. The Hague: Mouton.

Shannon, Claude, and Warren Weaver
1949 *The Mathematical Theory of Communication*. Urbana: University of Illinois Press.

Shapiro, Michael and Marianne
1976 *Hierarchy and the Structure of Tropes*. Lisse: The Peter de Ridder Press.

Shukman, Ann
1976 "The Canonization of the Real: Jurij Lotman's Theory of Literature and Analysis of Poetry", *PTL* 1, 317-38.

Solženicyn, Aleksandr
1968 *V kruge pervom*. New York: Harper and Row.

Spencer, Herbert
1875 *The Philosophy of Style*. New York: Appleton.

Stepanov, Jurij S.
    1971   *Semiotika*. Moscow: Nauka.
Šubnikov, A. V.
    1951   *Simmetrija i antisimmetrija konečnyx figur*. Moscow.
Taranovski, Kiril
    1953   *Ruski dvodelni ritmovi*. Belgrade.
Uznadze, Dmitrij N.
    1966   [1961] *The Psychology of Set*, trans. Basil Haigh. New York: Consul-
            tants Bureau.
Valentine, C. W.
    1962   *The Experimental Psychology of Beauty*. London: Methuen.
Valéry, Paul
    1957   "Poésie et pensée abstraite", *Oeuvres I*, 1314-39. Paris: Gallimard.
            [Article first published in 1939.]
Vološinov, V. N.
    1973   [1930] *Marxism and the Philosophy of Language*, trans. Ladislav
            Matejka and I. R. Titunik. New York: Seminar Press.
    1976   [1927] *Freudianism: A Marxist Critique*, trans. I. R. Titunik and ed.
            with N. H. Bruss. New York: Academic Press.
Voznesensky, Andrey, and Stanley Kunitz
    1972   "Voznesensky and Kunitz on Poetry", *New York Times Book Review*
            (16 April), 38.
Waryas, Carol L.
    1973   "Psycholinguistic Research in Language Intervention Programming:
            The Pronoun System", *Journal of Psycholinguistic Research* 2, 221-37.
Weyl, Hermann
    1949   *Philosophy of Mathematics and Natural Science*, revised and aug-
            mented English edition based on a translation by Olaf Helmer.
            Princeton: Princeton University Press.
    1952   *Symmetry*. Princeton: Princeton University Press.
Wilden, Anthony
    1968   *The Language of the Self*. Baltimore: Johns Hopkins Press.
Woodrow, Herbert
    1909   "A Quantitative Study of Rhythm", *Archives of Psychology* 14. New
            York: Science Press.
Zareckij, V. A.
    1965   "Ratim i smysl v xudožestvennyx tekstax", *Trudy po znakovym
            sistemam* 2, 64-75.
Zipf, G. K.
    1949   *Human Behavior and the Principle of Least Effort*. Cambridge:
            Addison-Wesley Press.

Index

SUBJECTS

STUDIES IN SEMIOTICS

Thomas A. Sebeok, *Editor*

1. Eugen Bär, *Semiotic Approaches to Psychotherapy.* 1975. xxx, 177 pp. ISBN 90 316 0116 0. Dfl. 33.–/$12.00

2. Mieczysław Wallis, *Arts and Signs.* 1975. x, 102 pp. ISBN 90 316 0117 9. Dfl. 16.50/$6.00

3. Roman Jakobson, *Coup d'oeil sur le développement de la semiotique.* 1975. iv, 23 pp. ISBN 90 316 0118 7.
Dfl. 5.50/$2.00

4. Richard A. Fiordo, *Charles Morris and the Criticism of Discourse.* 1977. viii, 197 pp. ISBN 90 316 0119 5.
Dfl. 30.–/$12.00

5. Thomas A. Sebeok, *Contributions to the Doctrine of Signs.* 1976. xiii, 271 pp. ISBN 90 316 0120 9. Dfl. 42.50/$17.00.

6. Adam Kendon, *Studies in the Behavior of Social Interaction.* 1977. viii, 260 pp. ISBN 90 316 0121 7. Dfl. 47.50/$19.00

7. Roberta Kevelson, *The Inverted Pyramid: An Introduction to a Semiotics of Media Language.* 1977. viii, 137 pp. ISBN 90 316 0123 3. Dfl. 30.–/$12.00

8. Michael and Marianne Shapiro, *Hierarchy and the Structure of Tropes.* 1976. v, 37 pp. ISBN 90 316 0135 7. Dfl. 8.75/$3.50

9. Roberta Kevelson, *Inlaws/Outlaws: A Semiotics of Symbolic Interaction: "Robin Hood" and the "King's Law".* 1977. v, 100 pp. ISBN 90 316 0136 9. Dfl. 15.–/$6.00

13. Harvey Sarles, *After Metaphysics: Toward a Grammar of Interaction and Discourse.* 1977. 286 pp. ISBN 90 316 0134 9.
Dfl. 45.–/$18.00

THE PETER DE RIDDER PRESS
P.O. Box 168, Lisse, The Netherlands